WOMEN I'VE LOVED

Lessons from friendships that changed a life

Romney Humphrey

INTRODUCTION

Each friend represents a world in us, a world possibly not born until they arrive, and it is only by this meeting that a new world is born.

Anaïs Nin

F riends play a huge role in the lives of most women. While my life has been no exception, my appreciation of companions is more intense than most.

As an only child with a particularly solitary and isolated life, my up-bringing was unusual, even for a child with no siblings. Because my dad was an airline pilot, we moved constantly. Never had contact with my only two cousins until I was fully grown. No aunts. Two strange uncles, both with significant personality disorders. An alcoholic and lackluster grandfather out of state and one nice grandmother, also out of state, both of whom I rarely saw.

I can't remember half the places we lived, but what I do recall vividly was the loneliness I felt every day. I was a quiet child with no self-confidence, so I wasn't like most other army brats who somehow quickly figure out how to make friends or alliances in new environments. That, paired with the fact that even when home, because of family dynamics, I was often alone in my room, contributed to my emotional isolation.

The lack of a brother or sister was an ache I never shook. Just to have a companion in a house that centered around adults, someone to talk to, even to fight with, seemed to me to be the ultimate blessing and luxury. I recall feeling a twinge in my heart when I would hear another child say "my brother" or "my sister" casually. Did they know what a privilege that was?

The result of those collective factors often felt like I was in a cage on the sidelines of other children's and families' lives. Watching, wanting, wishing for company, for a companion, for an alliance.

So, though most women value their friendships as one of the great riches in life, my friends have been, for most of my life, much, much more to me. They weren't just companions; they were a lifeline. Not merely a diversion; but entertainment, education and a window to the world. Not just comfort; but solace and joy. My friends became my sisters and my salvation, not once or twice, but throughout my maturation and beyond. Even when I had formed as a person, those girls and women who would impact my life acted as compensatory conduits for what most children receive via family life, siblings, school or neighborhood interaction.

By no means did I have a horrible upbringing compared to so many, but it was, I've realized over the years, unusual in social and familial gaps. How lucky I was to have so many females who nurtured, encouraged, instructed and modeled life practices and philosophies so I could adapt what I'd learned and grow as a girl and woman.

These are the stories of some of those women who came into my life. The ones I have chosen to write about floated like bubbles into my field of vision. There are many close friends not included here. I don't love them less, but each of the women and girls presented in this book uniquely moved me, one way or another, along the timeline of my soul, the formation of my psyche.

This book is about the lessons I learned, and the knowledge I acquired. It is how they formed the best of me.

CONTENTS

1

Ellie

But nothing makes a room feel emptier than wanting someone in it.

—Calla Quinn, *All The Time*

I n the years from kindergarten through third grade, my mother, father and I moved nine times. Seattle, California, Alaska. Alaska, Seattle, California. California, Alaska, Seattle. My father was a pilot, a partial motivation, but he also had a restless soul, so the moves were a mainstay of our lives.

My memories of the Alaska stays are clotted with running away from monster mosquitos in summer and carrying ice skates to school each wintertime day so I could skate on a giant pond in the playground during recess. I recall an oppressive shade of darkness in the mornings and evenings that furiously blanketed the frigid air. A distinct memory is of the moment I looked through a window caked with ice to see the black nose of a giant moose and its steadfast, sleepy eyes inches away staring back at me,

In California, I was awed by the beautiful dark skin of my Mexican American classmates, the first children of color I'd ever met. Another carryover was the experience of sitting on the grass beneath wet sheets as my grandmother hung them to dry, inhaling the specific scent of sunshine caressing clean, wet laundry. California was also my first experience of the pleasurable sensation of heat on my body and face—an opportunity Alaska and Washington never provided.

Because of so many moves and my inherent shyness, I'd never made a friend. Instead, I developed the habit of following other children out to recess, to the lunchroom and classrooms that never became familiar. This was my version of socialization, the only tool I had in my limited experience of social protocol. At home, I was often alone in my room (it was an unspoken rule when my father was in the house that he and my mother were not to be bothered). I had never visited the houses of other children. Neither did any children knock on the door of wherever it was we were visiting during our brief puddle jumping tenures.

When we finally settled in Seattle for more than a few months, we returned to a family neighborhood called Laurelhurst. The house was red with a turreted roof. As a child, I believed our house looked like a castle because of that small section that was distinctly different from neighboring abodes. Hardly a castle; just a two-bedroom, one bath house, but exotic in my five-year-old mind.

That neighborhood, now a highly desirable destination for families in the Northwest because of its proximity to the University of Washington and lakeside views, was where I lived when I made my first friend.

Ellie Smith lived at the end of our block with her brother Doug and, of course, their parents. She was a year younger than me, with corn-white hair a la Dutch boy framing a slightly chubby face and blue eyes that seemed to always be in half-blink. Her brother was the visual counterweight, with dark hair and eyes. He was thin and energetic, Ellie laconic and watchful. I realized later that she was very shy but that was my wheelhouse also, so she seemed 'normal' to me.

This was in the mid-nineteen fifties, and most houses on the block had a television in their front rooms. Ours did not, as my father had strong opinions about the 'boob tube', and I was jealous of the other kids on the block's viewing freedom. This was compounded by my yearning for Saturday cartoons and the phenomenon of The Mickey Mouse Club.

More than cartoons, though, television came to represent what brothers and sisters did together, and the pairing of those two riches was not only unattainable for me, but painful in the hopelessness of knowing I would never have either.

My envy must have been palpable, as I, five years old, was somehow invited one Saturday morning to trudge down the block to the Smith's house where Ellie cheerfully opened the door. This was the first time I'd gone to another child's house for entertainment or social interaction, and I was not, for some reason, terrified. Instead, I was giddy with anticipation for the revelation of the Mickey Mouse Club and the chance to sit beside another child and share the experience.

My memories of Ellie and her family center around the sense of contentment I immediately felt in subsequent Saturdays upon walking directly into their living room. None of the homes in the block had a formal entryway, as I recall, and certainly my parents' home and the Smith home did not. Yet there was a transition as I entered their home, as if I had walked through an invisible shield, once I ascended the five steps that led to their front door. Passing over their threshold made me immediately feel like a different sort of girl, one who did what other children did, one who was part of a real family for a time, one who could make believe that her life was different than the girl in the red house down the block.

Thus, I began to exist in two universes. During the week, I resided in our silent red house, my days after school filled with nothing but the few toys in my room or time spent in the rest of the house with my mother if my father was out of town. On Saturdays, I was part of a household filled with toys, noise and ongoing activity.

The contrast between the two worlds was even more dramatic on holidays and birthdays. In December, the Smith's house seemed to overflow with candy and presents. Candy was not allowed in the red house, and though my mother negotiated for a tree every year, the presents beneath its branches on Christmas morning were few and my stocking largely filled with oranges. It wasn't that my parents couldn't afford anything else; this was a deliberate lifestyle choice of my father's, and as the months progressed with me jockeying between the two households, the sight of the bounty of presents underneath the Smith Christmas tree that year filled me with a different kind of envy.

Ellie always shared her toys with me, almost as if she were merely the conduit for such treasures rather than the true owner of them. It made visiting her house like Christmas every day—all the dolls and games I would never have at my disposal at home. Yet, there was always that contrast.

I don't remember laughing much with Ellie, having secrets or embarking upon adventures of any sort. We just quietly played wherever we wished (another revelation). It got to the point that I would awaken early Saturday mornings, wait impatiently for my mother to stir, then race down the block without breakfast just to begin my morning with the family that now incorporated my presence into their weekends.

One year, Doug got a train for his birthday. Each railcar was filled with malted milk balls, a sight I had never imagined but one that filled me with glee. Candy wasn't just forbidden in our house; sugar was also viewed as evil, even in desserts, which were few and far between in the red house. The most common after dinner treat was baked apples, and that was a far cry from the everyday riches down the block. The sight of what seemed like an endless supply of malted milk balls was, in a sense, the most glorious sight my five-year-old eyes had ever seen. "Eat as many as you want," whispered Ellie, as always, sweetly generous. Once sanctioned, I *did* eat as many balls as I could stuff in my mouth. I returned home with a stomachache and no regrets.

Ellie's family also took me on my only trip to Disneyland. I don't recall the details but assume their family trip coincided with our concurrent visit to California to visit my father's mother in Glendale. My mother, father and I had never taken a vacation together, but here was a family who included me in a *real* family trip, as foreign an experience as the rides and sights of the magical destination.

Why in the world were those people so generous to include me in their Saturday mornings and that momentous trip to Disneyland? I have to believe they were just good people who recognized a nice social match for their shy daughter. Probably they felt sorry for me and my evident loneliness. Whatever the reason, their generosity afforded me the chance to feel like a normal child, and that gift made an indelible mark.

My first friend, a moon faced, open-hearted young girl, was an introduction to the power and sanctity of friendship. That beginning laid the foundation to a lifetime of girls and women who would, by virtue of their presence in my life, alter the trajectory of my social and emotional core.

2

Katie

A Different Kind of Girl

The free soul is rare, but you know it when you see it. Basically, because you feel good, very good, when you are near them.

—Charles Bukowski

I now had a friend, but it was a tentative beginning to feeling like a "regular" kid. Yes, Ellie's family were generous in their inclusion, but Ellie was so inward, as was I, that our time together was more a function of two bodies sharing a space or activity with no energy and virtually no interaction. More importantly, this entry into being, or appearing to be like other children, gave me a hunger for more.

I had begun to understand that there was more than one kind of child in the world. Ellie and I were quiet, her brother Johnny a bit more social, but I saw children at school who were constantly in motion, voices always at full strength, with energy that seemed to me like a constant source of pure fireballs. I didn't want to spend time next to those entities for fear of getting singed by their heat, but I liked noticing children different than Ellie and me. Now, rather than being in a cage on the sidelines, it was more like living in a zoo where I had a view of species similar to me, but wilder and more unpredictable. I was the timid little monkey in the corner, spending all day fascinated by the baboons.

In the lineup of houses on our street, accented by primrose trees that bloomed quietly and gracefully next to the sidewalk, Ellie's house was the last one on the block. My parents' home was three or four houses from the other end of the block. We had quiet neighbors, one couple with a Dalmatian named Sam who appeared to have no interest in anything or anyone in life; not cats, other dogs, and certainly not children. I was disappointed to have an animal so close with such little appeal.

In the middle of the block were friends of my parents who would remain in both of their lives long after they were divorced. Two houses down from them were the O'Malleys. This was a family of four children; a population that astounded me. If I felt the Smith house was active and cozy, the O'Malley home was pure chaos, filled with abandon on all fronts, whether it was the type of behavior allowed or practically unlimited access to food in the kitchen.

There was an older sister, Sarah, who was so consistently rude to any child who walked into the home I learned to scurry past her as quickly as possible. She was four or five years older than the next girl, Gail, who was followed in age by her brother Tom, just a year younger than her. And then there was Katie. I was six or seven when I met her; she a year younger.

I can't say that Katie was a friend, but she had a lot of impact on me. In my only-child emotional vernacular, for years I wondered if Katie and Ellie were sisters, even though they lived in different households. They had the exact same color of hair and eyes. Gail had red hair, Tom brown, and mean Sarah a blend of the two. Yet Katie, the youngest, sported the same wispy, flaxen hair that Ellie had, but the similarity ended there. Where Ellie was round, Katie was scrawny. Ellie was quiet, Katie was prone to wild laughter and unpredictable behavior.

This is how Katie formed me:

My "friend" experiences were clearly limited thus far in my young life since I had only a single frend: Ellie. That was it. Then, one afternoon, she led me into the O'Malley home. That resulted in occasional tagalong visits when Ellie or her brother ventured into that wild territory. One tremendous appeal of this jungle-like environment, with children sometimes literally hanging from various tops of doors like wild monkeys, was the free-for-all in their kitchen.

I was introduced to a whole new level of gustatory pleasure in the O'Malley kitchen. Where the Smith home offered plentiful candy, in the center of the O'Malley kitchen, the kids, visitors included, were allowed to open a bag of Wonder Bread (we only had whole wheat at our house), select as many pieces as they wished, then proceed to slather the heavenly offering with a generous layer of butter. That was topped with a dip into the sugar container, often with hands, occasionally a large tablespoon, to complete the extraordinary adventure. *Sugar!* On top of *butter!* On top of *Wonder Bread!* I was agog.

One day—it must have been a Saturday morning—I wasn't allowed much wandering license in the neighborhood during the week—after we'd all had our fill of the de rigueur house offering, Katie led us upstairs to a large attic room. She was still in her nightgown, and that casual mode of apparel for entertaining guests really impressed me.

"Line up there," Katie instructed, and the four or five of us, including Ellie and myself, obediently sat on the wood floor as Katie put a record on a small record player in the corner of the room. "I will now," she pronounced regally, "do a Can-Can for you." I had no idea what that would involve, but was quickly (and shockingly) educated.

Katie proceeded to kick her legs up in the air a la a six-year-old with no dance training. That was impressive enough, but the most astounding element of her performance was he attire: she wasn't wearing any underwear.

Well! At that point in my life, I don't think I'd seen my *own* nether region or that particular and blatantly exposed body part. And I certainly hadn't considered the possibility I might be introduced, in the most thrilling and shocking manner, to anyone else's. It was the first time in my childhood I remember getting that uneasy feeling of "Uh oh. I shouldn't be doing this."

Ellie and I exited fairly quickly. I'm sure she was as embarrassed as I was, but of course we didn't talk about it. Later, I came to regard Katie as a pioneer, a wild and willful spirit, and a hint of what a girl could *choose* to be.

Katie's contribution to my development was just that. Though I didn't have the guts or inclination to act as she had, that Can-Can established for me what would always be a fascination with wild girls and women completely different than me. If I couldn't *be* like that, I wanted to be in the same room, to watch and observe and somehow inhale the cellular discharge of those beings. I wanted to get a hit of that energy and abandonment, always hoping some of it would be somehow absorbed into my diet of proper and prim.

As it turns out, I had a few Katies in my life, and I am grateful for each one. But Can-Can Katie was my first and most memorable.

3

Jean

GENERATIONAL FRIENDS

Three things in human life are important. The first is to be kind. The second is to be kind. And the third is to be kind

—Henry James

The same block that claimed Katie and Ellie as inhabitants also housed the couple who were in my parent's social set. Jean and John had two boys, ten years apart, one of whom was somewhat my social peer. He was a quiet, artistic-leaning spirit who later became a graphic artist, but it wasn't Stuart that I was drawn to; it was his mother, Jean. She became my first friend of a different age, and one of the most important. I was approaching seven-years-old, still under the spell of Katie and the cushion of Ellie.

Jean was a tall woman, very slender, and would have been called "handsome" by her parents' generation. She was always beautifully groomed, but not flashy. Hers was a classic look, and she usually wore skirts with cashmere cardigans, buttoned down. Later, it would be slacks and those sweaters, but during most of my childhood, my memory is of tweed skirts and soft sweaters.

Jean owned a set of Oz books that she had been given as a child, and most had the date of the gift written in; mostly the early 1920's. Somehow, I learned that she read those books to Stuart on a regular basis, and either was sent to join the the duo by my mother or showed some initiative of my own. Regardless, I found myself sitting next to Jean, Stuart on the other side, being introduced to a world of Oz that far exceeded what the world knew from the very first book, *The Wizard of Oz*. There are fourteen Oz books that L. Frank Baum wrote, with many written by Ruth Plumly Thompson, but it was many of those first "real" Oz books that I heard, nestled next to Jean, transported by the adventures of Ozma, the Patchwork Girl, and all the colorful, magical characters that inhabited the world that Baum created.

But the reading was only a part of what caused me to love Jean. Jean was the first adult who showed an interest in me as a person. She asked me questions about what I thought about (not much of anything), what I'd been doing that day (again, not an impressive show) and generally asked my opinion about various subjects throughout our visits. She did this with Stuart also, and I learned much later in life, she did this with all the kids in the neighborhood who wandered into her house. But, I was the only one outside of Stuart that had the Oz sessions.

As I grew older, Jean remained in my life. Even after my parents were divorced Jean and my mother remained very close, and I would often see her and her husband John at my mother and stepfather's home.

John was a taciturn banker who'd often played silent games of chess with my father when they were neighbors. Once my mother moved and remarried, we discovered he wasn't a good match for my outgoing stepfather. But the two women still spent a lot of time together apart from their spouses, so Jean was one of the few females in my life I had a relationship with other than my mother. I had no aunts, two very strange uncles I never saw, and of course, no sisters.

My parents' divorce and my mother's remarriage were big adjustments in many ways, and I was to have a complicated relationship with my stepfather, a man who'd chosen my mother but wasn't thrilled with the rest of the package. We had moved to an island across a floating bridge from Seattle some distance from that old neighborhood, and of course I wasn't driving at that point, so time with Jean was far too limited.

By this point, Jean, a true intellectual with great warmth, would discuss books, films, political happenings and general topics of the day with me when we did get together. She still seemed amazingly interested in my opinion, and that was a powerful magnet. Even at thirteen and fourteen, I yearned to return to my childhood spot at Jean's side, listening to her beautiful voice as she applied significant acting talent, opening the door to Oz.

During one particularly difficult period of adjustment after my mother's marriage, my stepfather, began a subtle, passive aggressive campaign, sending me the clear message that I was a burden and a bother. This wasn't a new script for me; my father felt much the same, but his approach had been to ignore me. When my stepfather had been courting my mother, he'd been charming and inclusive, acting as if I was a wonderful add-on to the prize of my mother. I was entranced and excited; here was a father who wanted a daughter like me. His own daughter didn't live in the area and I had only met her once, so my role as the newly crowned, if not princess, then delight of the household, was available. It was seductive and exhilarating... and did not last longer than the first year after he moved into our house.

My stepfather was not a particularly clever man, so I have to believe he behaved this way by way of his subconscious. He had begun messaging me of his feelings by expelling heavy sighs when as I entered a room, interrupting any contributions I tried to make to a conversation, or regarding me with such disdain when I attempted to join in with him and my mother, I was usually prompted to turn around and retreat. I was devastated by the change in his approach and attitude towards me, and my mother wasn't able to offer comfort. Rather, she kept telling me I was "too sensitive"—a refrain I would hear for the rest of my life.

One afternoon, he added biting criticism about an opinion I'd offered, so unkind and blatant I couldn't ignore the intent. Aching with unhappiness and unable to go to my mother for solace, I left the home of my stepfather. The door didn't slam behind me; I was still too timid to stand up for myself. I walked to the house of a girl I knew slightly from the school bus and knocked on the door. The girl, Linda, who had the most beautiful hair I've ever seen, straight out of a Breck commercial, answered, perplexed.

"Can I use your phone?" I asked. Linda was puzzled - we'd barely spoken in all the years I rode the bus with her, but she allowed me in the house. These were the days when families only had one phone, so it was bit of a bold request. I called the number I'd memorized for years. "Jean, I want to come visit you. Right now." There was a pause on the other end of the phone.

"What's wrong?" she asked.

"Roy is being—"and I broke down in tears. Jean then instructed me to hand the phone to Linda's father, somehow arranging to order a taxi for a sum that would not be insignificant.

I arrived at Jean' house, she paid the taxi, and I fell into her arms, sobbing with all the angst a pre-adolescent could muster. She called my mother and arranged for me to spend the night, returning me the next morning. I recall her pulling my mother aside as I walked down to my room, leaden in my return, softly explaining my version of the situation.

My stepfather was a bit kinder after my dramatic journey, and Jean remained a beacon of hope and escape for me. Once I could drive, and for the rest of my adult life, I visited and phoned her. At one point, she gave me her collection of Oz books; one of the most meaningful gifts I have ever received. Clearly, my attachment to the books and what they represented was evident, and I'm sure Stuart didn't mind.

I often return to the books and re-read them. I still enjoy the writing and the stories, but it's the genesis of my introduction to that world that makes the visitation meaningful.

John died in his sixties and Jean remained alone for years. Then, in her late seventies, she met a wonderful man, a far better match for her than John, and they married. She was giddy in love, glowing with her good fortune, and he seemed to recognize the treasure he'd found in return. At their wedding, I, like a protective aunt, pulled the gentleman aside.

"You'd better take good care of Jean," I instructed sternly.

"I plan on it," he kindly answered.

Those few years of marriage so late in life, before Jean passed away, were very happy for her. She got the partner she deserved, even if it was for too brief a time.

Jean's impact on my life was monumental, and her friendship deeply meaningful. She taught me many things, including the value of having a friend from another generation. I would have a couple of those in my life, and now I am the "elder", but she was the first. I miss her still, many years after her death, as does everyone who knew and loved her. I am hoping she bequeathed me more than the Oz world. I like to believe that her legacy of grace and kindness in friendship is something I have extended to the children I taught and those of the generation after me.

4

Peggy

FIRST TIME CHOSEN

Friendship improves happiness, and abates misery, by doubling our joys, and dividing our grief

—Marcus Tullius Cicero

nnette's departure made life at the hotel lackluster, and I was glad when we moved to the island. It was a bit of a rocky transition. We stayed in an apartment, rented a house, then finally moved to a log home my father had been building. It was from a company called Pan Abode—they're still in business—and this was probably the only such structure at that time on an island that was on its way to becoming one of the wealthiest suburbs of Seattle.

The log cabin was set amongst the trees, with views of Lake Washington. Next door lived a family with a boy my age and his older sister—so much older I don't think I ever exchanged words with her. I had been excited to hear there was a child nearby, as this was not the density-rich offering of the city in terms of entertainment - Can-Can dances, cartoons, or otherwise. But the boy, Archie, was only interested in reptiles. Literally. Their basement was filled with glass aquariums housing various snakes and lizards. I *do* recall going to Archie's house one time to play cards, but the biggest takeaway from that experience was his father's insistence on showing us a scar on his stomach from the Korean war.

"Look at this," he directed, pulling up his shirt to display a jagged marking surrounded by a fair amount of belly fat. I remember being shocked he was so bold in displaying the evidence of his soldiering. We did not employ such casualness next door. "And, can you do this?" he added, rolling his stomach like a Balinese dancer.

"No," I whispered. Archie stared off in the distance. He'd seen this show numerous times. I avoided the house after that.

At this point, I was in third grade. Outside of Ellie and Katie, two girls I'd probably not spent more than a few hours interacting with outside of television viewing or lurid dance recitals, I hadn't ever really played with other kids. When I would see children in the alley playing kick the can or running in and out of one another's houses, it was my job to observe, not participate. I was flummoxed by the rules and rituals of other children.

My mother must have recognized my growing social deficit and made a bold move to compensate. Just before we moved to the Baroness Hotel, while we lived in the Laurelhurst neighborhood with Ellie and Katie down the block, my mother tried to direct a play utilizing the kids on the block. The musical *Peter Pan* was big at that time, and she loved musicals, so somehow, she corralled a few of the O'Malley kids and Ellie to join the cast. A few weeks before, she had taken me to get a haircut. And I mean *haircut*. She'd directed the stylist to do a "boy cut"—a choice I had no say about, nor understanding of its eventual result. Yep—it was a "Peter Pan" cut, and I was immediately cast.

"I want to be Captain Hook!" Katie demanded after she was told someone else had the lead.

"All right," my mother agreed, and proceeded to hand Katie a potato masher. Then, she wrapped a kitchen towel around the hand holding the masher handle. Voila; Captain Hook! I'm guessing that Ellie was a pirate—it was OK to be a pirate in the chorus, and Gail, Katie's older sister and a child with more intelligence than the rest of us, was likely Wendy.

We had three or four rehearsals. Then the gang lost interest. It was an understandable response. My mother had no directorial skills, none of us knew the music nor wanted to sing in front of one another, and a timid Peter Pan somehow sealed the demise of the production.

This meant when we made the move to yet another school and house, I could begin again in my search for a friend. The initial few months were typical. From a distance, I yearned for companionship. I ached for a pal to join me on the playground or at lunch, but instead I just observed, once again, the lives of other children, trying to note social cues and skills.

Just go up to them and ask if they want to play foursquare, I'd tell myself. *Laugh when the other kids laugh.*

I began employing those rudimentary shadow behaviors. One day, another quiet girl with sea-glass aqua eyes approached me. "Would you like to come to my house to play?" she asked. *Would I!* I hadn't noticed her before, much the same as no one noticed me, but suddenly all I saw was Peggy. I began to study her behavior at school. She seemed completely at ease at recess and in class, joining in if she felt like it, never a leader but definitely welcome wherever she wished. *Maybe she can explain it to me,* I mused, hopeful I'd finally have a guide into the foreign world of play. At the very least, I'd have a friend.

She gave me her phone number so my mother could call hers, and arrangements for a Saturday visit ensued. When our car pulled up to Peggy's house, I could tell immediately it was a different kind of dwelling than any I'd seen before. In Laurelhurst, all the houses were pretty similar. Peggy's family house, upon first viewing, looked *humble.* In the front yard, bats, balls, and garbage cans countered one another like numbers on a clock. I was a bit afraid to enter, not knowing what was on the inside. But Peggy and her mother opened the door, waved me in, and my mother drove away.

If the playground was like another city, the inside of Peggy's house was like another planet. The main room contained the living room and kitchen, and there was a large table in the middle, covered with games in various stages of play, though no one was currently engaged. Two large aquariums lined a bookcase that housed, not books, but *more* games. It wasn't the O'Malley version of chaos, nor the abundant caloric feast of Ellie's home. This house felt more like a circus, and I was giddy with glee about what a humble home had to offer.

"What do you want to do?" Peggy asked me politely. Having no idea what one *did* when playing at someone else's house, I threw the option right back.

"Whatever you want," I said, mesmerized by the colorful fish that seemed as casual as the rest of the room, zigzagging in their enclosures with what looked like joy.

"Monopoly," she declared, thus opening the door to the wondrous world of games, just as Jean had introduced me to Oz. She was a patient teacher, but I was often distracted by the constant stream of brothers and sisters, *their* friends attached, who weaved in and around the main room as we played the game.

Some of Peggy's brothers (were there two? Four?) were teenagers, and I'd never been around a teenager. They entered the room with such velocity it felt like a truck had just crashed through the front door. These boys were loud, and typically hit Peggy as they passed her at the table, coming and going, and she socked them right back. I was terrified one of them would accost me. *Should I hit them back? What if I cry?* Luckily, I was ignored, and I began to ease into the climate of a culture I'd never experienced, but one I now yearned to join.

Peggy and I became fast friends that year, but I transferred to another school for fourth grade and didn't see her again until high school, when our social sets were a complete mismatch. Yet, in the year we were eight and nine, she became my first real *play* friend.

Peggy allowed me a glimpse into a household that seemed to thrive on fun in every form, ongoing verbal and physical contact as part of daily discourse, and a chance to breathe in a completely different way.

When I was with Peggy, and particularly in her home, possibility was always in the air; a game, a change of venue, crazy snacks and hitting teenagers. It was as if, in her presence, and in that unassuming house, I had been newly released from my cage. She was a real friend, but also like a *vacation*.

As I grew older, I'd be gifted with other female friends whose company came with its own atmosphere. When I was in Peggy's circus house, it felt like my chest was lighter, unburdening me from my restricted sensibilities.

And, Peggy, my third friend, was the first companion who seemed to want to be with me for *me*—whomever that was—rather than a circumstantial friend. *That* gift was significant. I couldn't have named it, but being chosen, truly chosen, was revelatory. I had yearned for such an experience without understanding what the yearning was.

5

The Clique

GABBY AND DEB

Not belonging is a terrible feeling. It feels awkward and it hurts, as if you were wearing someone else's shoes.

—Phoebe Stone, *The Romeo and Juliet Code*

The next few years involved a new school every September. Not, as was typical prior to moving to the island, because my father thought the next, new house would make for a happier life for himself, but because the area was growing rapidly and impacting school boundaries.

I left Peggy behind mid-year in third grade for a transfer. I didn't make a friend at my new school the rest of that year but I did somehow develop a talent for tetherball.

I wasn't a physically active child or athletic in any regard, but somehow that recess pursuit was well suited to someone with reasonable eye-hand coordination and a deficit of friends. You didn't have to ask anyone to play with you, nor did you need an invitation; the practice was to stand in line—anyone could do it—and take a turn playing the champion of the moment.

That spring and into the next year, my "friend" was a pole, heavy rope and tetherball. I greeted that threesome with joy every recess because it took away the stress and loneliness of the playground. I didn't care if I lost; I could just get in line again. It didn't mean I had to be perceived as friendless; just that I wasn't as good as the boy or girl at the helm.

Amazingly, because it was the only pastime I engaged in every single recess, unlike the well-rounded children who spent their time outdoors doing a variety of things with various other kids, I became quite good at the sport. At my fifty-year high school reunion, someone actually mentioned the day I, a third grader, beat a sixth-grade boy—my only lifetime significant sports accomplishment.

Fifth grade and sixth were comprised of a new transfer each year. No time to find a Peggy, or even an Ellie. The only marked female bonding experience of a sort was in fifth grade. The vehicle? The MENSTRUA-TION film.

For weeks, there had been whispers about something important *just for girls.* Finally, on a Friday afternoon, the drama unfolded. All the boys were asked, in a solemn, near church-like cadence by our regular male teacher, to leave the classroom. The minute the door was shut, in came a *female* teacher and another classroom of girls-only. The female teacher, with the flair of a magician in training, turned out the lights and started up the projector. There, in a roomful of two classrooms worth of girls, we heard the gruesome, unimaginable truths about our body's future.

Of course, at recess immediately afterward, the boys, like bees swarming the juiciest stamen *ever,* pestered all the girls for information about what happened when they were forced out of their territory. No one asked me, of course, and for once, I was glad to be an outsider.

In sixth grade, I discovered boys. Well, one boy, Bob McArthur, and spent the majority of my time in school and until bedtime, worrying if he liked me. This pastime filled up an entire school year. Tetherball still occupied my body, but Bob invaded my mind.

In seventh grade, at that time on the island, students started junior high, and that transition meant that everything shifted. By this time, my parents had been divorced nearly two years. My mother and I lived alone in the log cabin, and within a year she would marry my stepfather and he would move into the house with her (us, sort of) while they built a new home a few blocks away. There were a lot of transitions at home and at school, the biggest of which was *cliques.*

Suddenly, at school, there weren't "best friends" meeting at recess or sitting across the cafeteria table from one another at lunch. Before, my worry had been about finding *one* friend. Now, I was anxious about finding a *group.* Now, the girls (and boys) moved in gatherings of three, four, and five. The energy accelerated, the noise level increased, and there was, not like good old menstruation, a *sexual* tension to *everything.* Now, it was how fast Group One passed Group Two's lockers or who stared at whom during class, followed by seven notes to *their* gang about the interaction. It was exhausting.

I had no friend, and no group. I knew which group I wanted to join, of course, and that was the Popular Girls. I don't know why I held such an ambitious aspiration, certainly my history hadn't indicated that there the slightest justification that this was a reasonable dream, but dream I did.

The Popular Girls were anchored by two alpha females; Gabby and Deb. They were both smart, they both exuded the confidence of four-star generals, and they both wore pointed saddle shoes.

This was just one pivotal issue with my dream: I had rounded saddle shoes. My mother had purchased them for me prior to the school year because she'd heard that's what the girls in junior high wore. They did. But, unfortunately for me, graduating from sixth grade to seventh meant that one turned in, or threw away, their rounded saddle shoes and up-graded to the pointed. My mother didn't get that memo, nor did she fall prey to my tearful pleas for replacing the grade school version for the junior high version. I'd worn the shoes; we couldn't take them back. And she didn't have the funds nor openness to the whims of a twelve-year old to succumb to my constant, miserable attempts at negotiation.

I tried scuffing the shoes to death. No. Putting the shoes at the back of my closet. Absolutely no. I was stuck with wearing those *baby* shoes to school and experienced a walk of shame every time I had to pass Gabby and Deb in their glamorous, upgraded footwear.

One day (and I don't know how I got so bold) I decided to write a note to Deb. I had seen that note writing was standard communication fare for all the kids, not just the popular girls, so, using my very best handwriting, (that was another thing about those two; their handwriting was off-the-charts beautiful), I said something like, "Want to be friends?"

Oh, yes, something like that. That's pretty much what Peggy had said to me three years earlier, with great success, so it was the only familiar color in my rudimentary crayon box. And, for some unexplainable reason, Deb found this innocent query to be entertaining, and invited me to *the table.*

I joined the Popular Group at lunch that day, Deb making room for me, acting as if it were nothing—no big deal—having no idea that my greatest fear now was that I might wet my pants from excitement once I sat on the unforgiving slats of hard plastic attached to the lunch table.

I managed to contain both my body and my verbal output, somehow, if not contributing, at least playing at participating in the conversation. By now I'd become a great mimic and was a quick study, a la a co-dependent, hypersensitive and alert being (a skill that, under the tutelage of an alcoholic stepfather, would be honed to perfection in years to come) so I was, miraculously, integrated into the group.

My saddle shoes became the "in" joke, and I laughed expertly with the rest of them about my mother's cluelessness. I threw her under the bus faster than a wink from a seventh- grade boy, and never turned back.

Deb and Gabby stayed close friends throughout junior high, and we all remained connected for decades, sometimes closer, often distant, but always somehow bonded. Gabby and I reconnected when our children were young and we shared many wonderful times together with our families. In our sixties, circumstances changed dramatically, and the friendship ended. Deb never married or had children, and we, too, lost touch.

There are only a few friendships I've had in my life that ended abruptly or dramatically, and those "Popular Girls"—a clique, if you will—are in that sad, yet distinct category. But the loss, for me, doesn't negate my gratefulness for their openness to my wish to join their group, to be incorporated into what had become the social norm—a gigantic transition: Not one friend, but *some* friends.

This initiation led me to the experience, and then concept, of friendship within a group. Today, different clusters I've known and formed are the anchors, in many ways, of my emotional well- being outside of my husband and family. And I will always, *always*, appreciate that those two girls, for whatever reason, let the outsider with the wrong shoes into the room.

6

Snow White

Some birds are not meant to be caged, that's all. Their feathers are too bright, their songs too sweet and wild. So you let them go, or when you open the cage to feed them they somehow fly out past you. And the part of you that knows it was wrong to imprison them in the first place rejoices, but still, the place where you live is that much more drab and empty for their departure.

—Stephen King, Rita Hayworth and *Shawshank Redemption*

The summer after seventh grade, the year of Gabby and Deb, I went to camp for the first and only time. I was twelve, nearly thirteen, and most of the counselors were just a couple of years older than me. Campers were typically six or seven through twelve years old, so the fact that I began my short career as a camper as a "senior citizen" was due, I am quite sure, to a well-plotted scheme by my stepfather to remove me from the household for as long as possible.

Acquiescing, my mother got busy learning about options. She wasn't really connected to the parents of my schoolmates, still socializing with Jean across the lake or volunteering reading for the blind, so I'm not sure how she located a camp that included campers of my awkward age. She persisted, and Camp Armac, a good hour and a half drive away from my stepfather's house, met the requirements.

My mother packed for me as per the camp checklist and threw in a couple of sanitary napkins along with jeans, one candy bar, and two new sweatshirts. I was twelve and hadn't had my period, so, despite the introduction to the phenomenon via the fifth-grade FILM, I was alarmed by the inclusion of the materials.

"Why are these here?" I asked, embarrassed.

"You never know," my mother shrugged.

I was terrified someone would see the telltale sign of potential womanhood in my little suitcase, but I was not, as usual, in control of anything, so stuffed them inside the sleeve of one of the new sweatshirts.

My mother drove me to the camp, walked me to the main office, and gave me a hug good-bye. I'm sure this was difficult for her—the pressure from my stepfather to create a life focused on the two of them an ongoing campaign—but she was upbeat about what a great experience I would have. I was already planning to get sick the next day, requiring her quick return, so gave her a brave smile as I saw her walk slowly to her car.

I carefully unpacked my few "camp clothes" and placed them into the two drawers that had been allocated, hiding the sanitary napkin under the sweatshirts at the bottom of the drawer. Then, I waited for other campers to arrive, hoping, but not expecting I'd find a like-minded pal to help me through the next two weeks.

My primary concern was that the other girls my age—if there were any - would not know I had been a part of the popular group at my local junior high. I already knew if I somehow aligned myself with another camper, it wouldn't be a lasting friendship—it was very doubtful anyone else at Camp Armac sat at the Popular Girls' table at their school—*that* kind of status was not easily acquired.

Some younger girls, clearly close friends, wandered in and giggled their way to a set of bunk beds. I had claimed a bottom bunk, as I was, even then, a neurotic scaredy cat and was sure if I slept in a top bunk I would fall, die, and never see my mother again.

A dark-haired girl appeared in the doorway, and I did a double take. She was from my school—my very same school. A look of recognition was exchanged between the two of us—sort of *well, you'd be all right if no one better comes along* silent agreement. The girl's name was *not* really Snow White, but she had a name not dissimilar, recognizable via a well-known children's tale. It was such an unusual delineation, revealing, in some inexplicable way, how odd her parents were to burden a child with such a name in that manner, but Snow White it was. This familiar, but not familiar girl, now at Camp Armac, quietly settled herself into the bunk above mine.

Snow White, to be clear, was *not* in the Popular Girl group at our school. The burden of her name was so pronounced, she was constantly being ridiculed. She seemed a chirpy sort, though, and used to such harassment. She appeared to, if not rise above the taunting, tolerate it well. She didn't have a clique of her own but managed to maintain a watchful, hopeful air as she interfaced with various other outsiders. However, I *was* concerned that, if we associated at camp, she might expect a carryover to the next school year, so proceeded cautiously. No commitment was made, but there was an unspoken "I'll be your backup if you need one." The possibility of finding someone else to align with at camp seemed slim; we were the oldest in our now-full cabin and the next age group up were the counselors-in-training.

My worries about cementing a commitment with Snow White and the potential complications in the following school year were quickly trumped by what happened the next morning. As I sat on the toilet—one I found foul and painfully public (one of the few advantages of being an only child is you don't have to share a bathroom) I went to pull up my underpants and found—blood.

Yes, my mother had somehow intuited, however young I was for this transition, my first period. I was devastated, scared, and immediately teary. I *kind* of knew what to do with the sanitary napkin, but not really.

I wanted to be home with my mother, sure that confessing the situation to a camp official would be tantamount to death by shame. I quickly stuffed some toilet paper in my pants and went to find Snow White.

She was sitting on the top bunk, knees hanging over, looking about her with that same optimistic openness I'd seen so often at a distance. "Snow White," I whispered, and gestured for her to join me ground level.

She lightly descended the ladder.

"What?"

"Have you ever—uh—you know."

"No. What?"

"Had your—*period?*"

"I'm only twelve. Of course not."

Then, she looked at my face, the tears, the terror. "Oh," she said.

"Do you know how to put on one of those belts?" I asked.

"I saw that film. I can figure it out," she answered, matter of fact.

Snow White proceeded, upon my direction, to remove the equipment required from beneath my sweatshirt, follow me into the narrow stall of the bathroom, and hook up the apparatus. Suddenly, my concern about her status at school dissolved, and she became, in that instant, a friend.

We spent the two weeks dutifully following the camp regimen. It wasn't exactly fun; I yearned to return home early, but it was, thanks to Snow White, tolerable. I finished my period and told her I would help her when the time came. Strangely, she was one of the last of my acquaintances to achieve that developmental milestone—not until she was fifteen.

When the school year began, I was prepared to vouch for Snow White's legitimacy as acceptable, socialize with her, (outside of the cafeteria, which was sacred ground) and always honor her confident willingness to assist me in my time of need. My vow was never challenged. Snow White remained apart from all the groups, still positive, still openhearted, always greeting me with a smile. *We did something together and survived, didn't we,* we radioed as we passed in the hall.

Throughout high school we maintained the same *I know you but don't worry* distance. Then, when we were sophomores in college and attending the same state university, we both signed up for a semester abroad. I had done so because my best friend Laurie had enrolled, and I went wherever Laurie went, including to that particular university. Snow White was a French major and had always planned for the experience.

Laurie cancelled last minute, and I found myself, again, though this time in the beguiling location of Avignon, France, in strange territory with Snow White the only familiar, and now dependable, source of companionship. But in Avignon, something extraordinary happened. Snow White, who'd never found a social niche, blossomed in every possible way. Always a cute girl, now her dark hair, piquant features and positive energy vibrated. No longer a bouncy cheerleader, (somehow despite her social isolation she captured that title—it was like everyone recognized her earnestness) Snow White transformed into a stunningly beautiful young woman.

The members of our group found themselves constantly drawn to her—not just for her captivating looks, but her *presence*. It was like she'd been ignited from within. Her French was excellent, and she immediately befriended the locals, including a watchmaker with whom she had a brief affair. It was as if that positive outlook and constant openness all those years had been a bank Snow White had contributed to, penny by penny, and now the vault was overflowing, the investment having dramatically, and somehow magically, compounded.

One day, we were on an excursion, part of our weekly curriculum in that gorgeous part of Provence. Snow White and I sat together in the bus, and I felt lucky to have been chosen as her companion. We'd all packed lunches, and as we ate, she pulled an orange out of her bag and held it up.

"Look at this," she said, awe holy in her voice. She began to peel the orange. Then, once denuded, she held it up for my perusal. "Isn't this the most amazing thing you've ever seen?" she asked. "Look at the veins. The color. Now," she said, as she extended me a portion, "taste the juice, and when you do, remember that color, and those veins, and where it came from—all for you, and for me, in this moment."

This girl, at the peak of her beauty and consciousness, transported and elevated my perceptions on that bus, somehow delivering the kind of awareness that usually comes with a substance-altering drug. She did so with her essence, now like a constant, vibrant glow, but also with that same core of confidence that had rescued me so many years before.

Sadly, so sadly, that spring in Provence triggered something in Snow White. We both returned to our pedestrian campus in the fall, no longer immersed in the romance and thrill of life in France. The adjustment was difficult for me at first, but I quickly returned to the rhythms of college life. Snow White's transition was different. It was brutal, as if she'd been hurtled into the heavens, cavorted with angels, claimed her rightful place in the universe, then had been maniacally grasped by a dark, manacled hand and thrown into Hell.

She suffered a psychotic break, was diagnosed with bipolar disorder, and spent the next ten years bouncing from manic high to horrid low, giddy to desperate, captivating to distressing. Eventually, after a couple of attempts, she committed suicide by jumping off a building. Her rise and fall were particularly heartbreaking because I had seen her when she so joyfully claimed her true, rightful place on earth. When she was gone, my sadness at the sentence of her disease was sweetened by remembering her in her glory. The orange, the enchantment of that moment.

The final lesson from my friend Snow White? Most of us muddle through, with our ups and downs, meeting challenges, experiencing disappointments, chalking up small glories. But there are a few of us who were meant for higher highs, and lower lows, and their journey is one that should inspire heartfelt empathy. Yet, there will be those moments, if we are by their side, when the brightness from their shining star lets us bear witness to gasp-inducing transcendence, and all we can do is bow in gratefulness for having been present in that glorious moment.

7

Laurie

The Girl Who Changed Everything

*But oh! the blessing it is to have a friend to whom one can speak
fearlessly on any subject; with whom one's deepest as well as one's most
foolish thoughts come out simply and safely. Oh, the comfort - the
inexpressible comfort of feeling safe with a person - having neither
to weigh thoughts nor measure words, but pouring them all right out,
just as they are, chaff and grain together; certain that a faithful hand
will take and sift them, keep what is worth keeping, and then with the
breath of kindness blow the rest away"*

—Dinah Craik, *A Life for a Life*

Eighth and ninth grade, in terms of friends, allowed me continued access to Deb and Gabby. I wasn't invited to *all* the sleepovers, and there were private jokes and references I never got, but overall, I was included.

Gabby and Deb attended make-out parties on a regular basis, could list an impressive number of boyfriends they'd accrued by the end of eighth grade, and were so sophisticated and worldly that I, with no boyfriends or other social resources, simply observed their junior high dramas with envy.

The island was growing so fast, that in our ninth-grade year, a new junior high was built. During the process, the two existing schools were juggled in a double shift configuration. We were "South" and attended in the morning. "North" had the afternoon session. Occasionally there would be a party that mingled kids from both schools, and it was at one of those that I met Laurie, who would change my life.

Laurie attended North, so I only met her a couple times before high school, but I was struck, as was anyone who saw her, with her singular appeal. She wasn't pretty; she was adorable, but in an unusual way. Short, but with distinctive features that included a slight cauliflower ear, pointed chin, small sapphire eyes and a squeaky voice, she somehow magically blended those deficits into assets. And though seemingly petite, she had notably muscular arms and legs, developed as a competitive water-skier during her childhood. It was widely known that Laurie was the most popular girl at North, friends with everyone, and on each boy's list of "Most Wanted" as a girlfriend.

On one of the first days of high school, at age fourteen, I saw Laurie in the hallway. She seemed open and friendly, and I responded in kind. Not long into our sophomore year, we began spending more and more time together.

That year, there was a "click" in my heart, triggered by the bond formed with this girl who had chosen me just as I had chosen her. We each had boyfriends throughout our high school years, but our lives centered around one another. As important as boys were at that point in our lives, at the end of the day, it was always Laurie who provided me with the most entertainment and joy from spending time in her company.

Laurie was several inches shorter than me, but we both had the same color of brown hair, worn long, and over those next few years our matching hairstyle created a perception that we were twins of a sort. It was as if our shared hair color and cut was a visible cue for the underlying alliance and simpatico of our connection.

My mother and stepfather had been married a year by that time, and Roy's continued aggrievement about my presence in the home was

36

pervasive. We had a dog that I'd been given when my parents were divorced, Pepi, and Roy quickly taught the cocker spaniel to move away from whatever room he occupied. Several times a day, Roy would say, "Other room" to Pepi, and she would obediently trot to the threshold of the next room. I knew, subliminally, he also wished for a similar displacement from me. He wasn't a bad person, just selfish and simplistically immature. He wanted my beautiful mother, period. He was civil when friends would visit the house, but his welcome always had an unspoken time limit.

I had always felt like an outsider when my parents were married. After the divorce, my mother and I had a year alone, followed by her inviting my grandfather to live with us. The latter situation was disastrous, so when my grandfather departed and Roy met my mother and courted her (and me) I was hopeful for a new beginning.

It only took a few months for that "outsider" role to return with a vengeance. I rarely saw my father, and of course had no siblings to ally with, so the sense of isolation and pure loneliness when at home was a constant. My mother was happy, finally secure financially and emotionally, but I was miserable.

Then, came Laurie. And, a reverse universe from the one I occupied in my stepfather's home.

Laurie lived fifteen minutes away with her parents, Jean and Russ, and her older brother, Benji, who was two years older than us. I carried within me a passionate crush for Benji throughout high school and college, which Laurie tolerated with good cheer.

Jean and Russ were fine, spirited people, with a close group of friends who loved cocktail hour and a good laugh. At Laurie's house, everyone— adults *and* teenagers, were included in everything, and that now meant I was part of the fray. Jean and Russ seemed to have presumed early on that I was Laurie's missing sister who had casually returned home for an extended stay. It was as if I had always been part of the household from the first time I walked in the door. If it was cocktail hour, Laurie and I sat and chatted with whomever was included. At dinner time, both of us were assigned our prep chores. If we came home from school together, Jean would want a full report from both of us.

The family had a second home at a nearby lake, a half hour drive away. It was a humble, three-bedroom, one bath cottage on the lake where Laurie and Benji had learned to waterski. They spent each summer at the lake, and now I joined them on a regular basis. This worked well for Roy, but it was also bliss to me. The first night I visited the lake house, Jean said, "Romney, you fill the taco bowls." I'd never had a taco, and when I told Jean this, she laughed and said, "You'd better learn, because around here, that's every Friday night."

Aside from Peggy's family that I'd observed less than ten times in the year we were pals, and Ellie's family's television gatherings, I'd never been around a "real" family for any length of time. Never witnessed full-on love for a child from two parents. Hadn't seen mothers and fathers laugh with their children as if it were part of their daily bread. As I began to spend most weekends and several days during the week at Laurie's family home, I was enfolded into the rhythms and freefall affection that formed the foundation of the household.

Laurie was just as good and generous as her parents. She was a steadfast friend, loyal and committed, and she modeled those qualities to me every moment we were together. I, in turn, so grateful not just for her friendship but for the family that now seemed to regard me as theirs, began to practice the basic, pure tenets of a real, true friendship.

Roy and my mother had never taken me on a vacation of any sort, nor had my mother and father. When my mother and Roy went on vacation, I was not included; they woud, leave me in the care of an unfamiliar college student or, if I was lucky, Laurie's family. Those were awkward, lonely times, under the charge of someone who didn't know me, with added restrictions to an already regimented structure at my stepfather's house.

That was another thing about the different environment at Laurie's; she had no restrictions. There was such a level of trust and understanding that she had no curfew, drove her own little jeep she shared with her brother once she was sixteen, and operated within perfectly reasonable expectations of common sense. In Roy's house, I had a strict curfew, study hours imposed (I was never a great student, and my unhappiness at home compounded the status) and, considering I was a good kid, I felt these laws were overly restrictive.

The freedom at Laurie's home just added to the grand ride I was having. Then, they invited me to join their family on their yearly Hawaiian vacation. Despite the usual restrictions, my step-father was more than happy for me to be away and allowed me to go.

This gave me the first and only family vacation of my life and I actually accompanied Laurie and her tribe two times. I learned of their long-standing custom of having coconut cream pie every night after dinner at a local coffee shop. I also learned how to swim in the surf, and what a really bad sunburn felt like.

Every day, Laurie and I would decide our plan for the morning and afternoon, and each evening we would join her parents and Benji for dinner. It was relaxed and joyful. There were times the five of us would walk down the street together and I would think, wondrously, *everyone thinks I'm part of their family.* The sense of belonging was so unfamiliar, it took me some time to identify the sweet emotion I was experiencing.

The Hawaii trip during our senior year was particularly heavenly, but there was a tinge of sadness too. I could now see, in the near future, that my brief life with a real family would, after leaving for college, develop into an adjusted, fractured version. I didn't want to grow up and move on. I wanted to nestle into the twin bed opposite Laurie's in her bedroom or hang out in that kitchen and living room I'd come to love. I just wanted to be with these extraordinary beings who'd created a sacred and joyful space for me to exist.

Those years alongside Laurie during high school, welcomed into every facet of her existence, were the happiest I'd had in my life. I followed Laurie to the college of her choice, and it was Jean and Russ who drove us there for our freshman year, just like sisters. Laurie is my friend still, nearly sixty years after our first meeting. I have repeatedly told her how she contributed to my emotional well-being during those difficult years, and she always looks at me with surprise. To her, what she offered, and what her parents provided, was just life; normal, standard fare. To me, though, the growth I made under that family's unconscious tutelage compensated for a number of challenging random and collective factors in my emotional makeup.

Laurie's friendship, and that of her family, was revelatory. It was sustenance, nurturing, and, ultimately, emotional salvation. I now had a launching pad for my next stage of life. Though my twenties would prove to be tumultuous, I often think that, if not for Laurie, they might have been disastrous. This pivotal friendship remains one of my most treasured, and the appreciation for its gift in my life immeasurable.

8

Diana

A REAL-LIFE EDUCATION

The first step to the knowledge of the wonder and mystery of life is the recognition of the monstrous nature of the earthly human realm as well as its glory, the realization that this is just how it is and that it cannot and will not be changed. Those who think they know how the universe could have been had they created it, without pain, without sorrow, without time, without death, are unfit for illumination.

—Joseph Campbell

Often, I think of my life as pre-Laurie and post-Laurie; her impact was so significant and defining. I had, during those intense years I spent with her, become the person I saw reflected in Laurie's eyes; what she expected and modeled. The inherent best of me was nurtured, helping to solidify my first sense of self.

Part of the grounding I received had to do with predictability; Laurie was always Laurie, her parents would envelop me into their family life, and I could count on all of that to continue. Now, at seventeen, I thought I understood the essence of a true friend; someone I could trust to be constant and reliable, to be whom I knew them to be. I assumed, when I acquired another close friend in the future, the rules and expectations would be the same.

With Diana, I learned otherwise.

When Laurie and I entered our freshman year at the university, she went directly to a sorority, I to a dorm. It was our first real separation in three years, and I missed her.

My dorm roommate and I were as mismatched a pair as one could conjure; she was painfully shy, highly religious and accomplished academically. I was a lackluster student, hoping to make new friends, learn how to smoke cigarettes, survive classes, and find a boy to love.

And though I missed Laurie, and would visit her often at the sorority, I was eager to bond with the twelve or so girls in the hallway of my dormitory (my roommate being the exception).

This was 1967, and our country was about to be invaded by the "hippie" movement, the Vietnam war, and drugs. But in Eastern Washington, campus life went on much as it had for decades. Girls wore skirts to class and sororities and fraternities were the social core. There was a purity about the place. One day, as I was walking across campus, I saw a boy carrying an umbrella upside down, looking up at the cloudless sky like a mime in training. It wasn't raining—he was making a statement about *something,* and I recall feeling uneasy. Anything outside of my *known* was frightening.

The girls in the dorm were my first introduction to a bit of diversity. Many smoked, many drank. Some came from working class homes—something not to be found on the island where I'd been living. Most intriguing, but also a cause for uneasiness, a few of the girls seemed knowledgeable about sex, and comfortable with casually peppering innuendos into their conversations. When I heard such references, I felt naïve and unsophisticated. I remember studying the duos from each room, trying to decode these exotic, foreign girls, so *informed* about aspects of life I hadn't even considered.

I felt most comfortable with Diana, an olive skinned, dark-haired and beautiful girl with a quiet, cheerful countenance. She was from a small town outside of Seattle and dating a boy she'd known since junior high. Though I was curious about those wilder girls who taught me to smoke and introduced me to beer, Diana felt most like home. I suppose she was comfortable for me because she seemed so similar to Laurie; a nice girl from a solid, loving family.

The summer after our freshman year, Diana and I visited one another in our parents' homes several times. Her mom and dad reminded me of Laurie's parents, always making me feel welcome. There was that same sense of a loving, light-hearted household. I came know Diana's boyfriend Mark, a cute boy with a wicked sense of humor. And though I still spent most of that summer with Laurie, the matchup with Diana felt like, if not a substitute for my high school friend, a meaningful connection. I was clear that I now knew Diana, and she, me, and I found comfort in the alliance and its future.

Laurie, Diana and I were to return to campus in the fall. I was to join Laurie in the sorority and Diana would remain in the dorm. But I knew I would see her on a regular basis. Then, on a summer day shortly before returning for our sophomore year, I got a call. The impact of it would be as memorable to me as the day in eighth grade when we heard over the loudspeaker at school that President Kennedy had been shot. This phone call from Diana wasn't anything on a national level, of course, but it was important, and shocking, in the personal realm.

"I'm pregnant," Diana said over the phone. "We're getting married and having the baby."

I was stunned. Firstly, because I wasn't sexually active, and it hadn't occurred to me that a good friend of mine would, or could, be. Diana was nineteen, pregnant, and soon to be married. This was not the standard of the times, or of the girls I'd known. Pregnancy wasn't what happened to "good girls", but Diana *was* a good girl. I was disappointed, then sad, but mainly bewildered. It was as if she'd announced she had enrolled in the Army and was going to war—it was that unexpected and out of character. By this time, she was one of my two emotional anchors—the girl I went to for fun, for comfort and advice. Now, she'd gone down a path so unfamiliar, I was unmoored.

The aftermath of that phone call and its consequences was that I learned, for the first time, that bad things, or at least very challenging things, happened to good people, people I knew and loved. Until then, I hadn't observed my peers confronting a major life roadblock. It was difficult to fully comprehend, and my reaction to the situation was diametrically opposed to Diana's. To me, someone hadn't followed the rules, or at the very least, had not behaved as I had expected. To Diana, an unfortunate circumstance was met with, after the initial shock, positivity, and joy. She acknowledged that the detour was significant but met it with good cheer and resolve.

At nearly nineteen, everything that happened in my daily and weekly life, whatever occurred, was always framed in high drama. Boyfriend breakup? The end of the world. Continued issues with my family? Surely no one else had ever been so maligned. Not accepted into the school of my choice? I was the world's biggest failure. Now, here was a *real* problem that I couldn't imagine facing, and furthermore, my friend wasn't responding in full catastrophe mode as I would have. To Diana, the pregnancy was simply an unfolding of an unexpected circumstance, something she handled with measured assurance. Part of her process was her strong faith, one that she and Mark shared. To her, God would show the path. Not having a religious background, that strategy seemed questionable to me.

Returning to campus that year after her daughter's birth, Diana's existence changed dramatically. Married student housing. Nursing a baby while her peers partied and dated. Adjustments had to be made to the timeline of her educational plan. Diana, strangely philosophical and cheerful, forged through it all.

Her experience provided me with an impactful life lesson. I understood now that, even with intimate friends, parallel life paths were not a given. Trajectories could –and would—change. Of course, that happens, developmentally, in one's twenties, but this was my first encounter with that particular reality a bit early in the timeline. I had been so protected in the womb of Laurie and her family, I truly had assumed that life would follow a formula; one of my choosing.

Now I understood I could no longer expect complete cohesiveness with the lives of chosen friends. When someone veered from the vision I had imagined for their life, or the role they would play in mine, I recognized the importance of being philosophical and empathetic, however perplexed I might be. The sky wasn't falling; the landscape was merely shifting. In modern parlance, everyone's journey is their own. Diana, in her steadfast, capable way, modeled maturity and self-responsibility, two qualifiers I could not claim for myself at the time.

To this day, things that would knock me to the ground only give Diana momentary pause. She has had many more devastating challenges, including a handicapped son and surviving cancer. Her spirit has weathered the loss of her husband of over fifty years. Throughout, when confronting major issues, she regards it as a situation where her faith and common sense calmly dictate her responses. There's always a sweet calm in her eyes and voice. It's like a crown, a mantle, of a woman who, in my eyes, despite the losses and heartbreaks, is a real-life queen—one who provided me a profound lesson, fully framed by grace, setting an example for how to meet the unexpected with strength and wisdom.

That pretty girl down the hallway in the dormitory turned out to be, not a disaster, not a failure, or disappointment, but a beacon.

9

Sooz

ATTITUDE ADJUSTMENT

Humor can make a serious difference. In the workplace, at home, in all areas of life—looking for a reason to laugh is necessary. A sense of humor helps us to get through the dull times, cope with the difficult times, enjoy the good times and manage the scary times.

—Steve Goodier

When I began to outline the chapters of this project and make a list of who has impacted me profoundly in my life, many of the females I selected revealed themselves immediately. Childhood influences were quite obvious, as were the girls from the years before college. But, pondering the effect of friends as I moved into my twenties and thirties required more discernment and thought.

Johann Wolfang von Goethe said, "Tell me with whom you associate, and I will tell you who you are." When I was twenty, I had a subliminal understanding that whomever I spent time with, men *and* women, would be a mirror, a reflection, of where I was, spiritually and emotionally. Hang with the high-flying party girls? It followed that I would be required to match them drink for drink. Start attending church with my old dorm roommate? No thanks and amen, but similar opportunities were still there. As far as female friendships, the young women I met now offered a varied menu of possibilities for different kinds of connections. Subliminally, I understood that these choices would inform how my character would continue to develop. And though many of my selections weren't specifically deliberate, they were now becoming more of a conscious choice.

Laurie and her family had helped to form me; Diana complemented my growth in awareness about certain aspects of life, but the young women who claimed their territory in the next couple of decades felt more like teachers of specific qualities and principles I would do well to emulate. And, a quality I sorely needed then, was humor and a sense of fun.

I met Sooz in the sorority. That experience was brief for me—I was itching for a much less traditional setting for my academic and personal growth, but Sooz came into my life just before I transferred to another school and has remained a beloved friend ever since.

Sooz was a college star. Pretty, artistic, with a beautiful singing voice and a constantly upbeat personality, she was the girl in our sorority everyone wanted as a friend. I wasn't a very confident student or social hit within or outside of the sorority, but Sooz, in contrast, was socially active in various groups, selected as Sweetheart of fraternities, and formed a cozy sub-culture of followers wherever she went.

She was always friendly, but I didn't really connect with her until the "smoking room." At that time on campus, smoking was common, but only allowed in designated places in our living accommodations. In our sorority, the smoking room was located on the ground floor, furnished with comfortable couches, chairs, and plenty of ashtrays. (Ick, right?)

I had acquired the habit in the dorm, so tentatively found my way to the room the first week I transferred to the sorority. I recall being shocked to see Sooz there. She was very feminine—actually ladylike—and most of the girls I saw in the smoking room were bold or slightly rebellious. Yet, there was proper Sooz, holding her cigarette like a 1940's movie star. I immediately adjusted my perception of the "perfect girl" and cottoned to her even more.

She didn't often visit the room (I was there constantly) but seeing her in that environment gave me the confidence to pursue the friendship outside that setting. Then, her boyfriend Gordy, who attended another college, formed an immediate bond with my current boyfriend on one of his visits, and that cemented the friendship.

Once I started spending more time with her, either one-on-one or with our boyfriends, I noticed that Sooz, no matter what the activity, always had fun. Not the fun of having a couple of beers, or the fun of telling jokes, but *everywhere* fun. It was like she was lighter inside, and had more room to enjoy each action, every word or circumstance.

I am *not* a fun person. I can be funny upon occasion, and I work very hard to *try* to be fun, but it does not come naturally. I am, at my core, a grump. As another friend (you will meet her in a future chapter) would say to me at age twenty-one, "Rom, it's like you're eighty years old!" Eighty, and *cranky*.

But Sooz was fun with *everyone,* particularly with Gordy. Part of their chemistry was their shared sense of humor—one that continues to be incorporated into their conversations after fifty years of marriage. Sooz also, being quick to laugh, somehow makes *other* people funnier. You know that person that makes you feel wittier and somehow inspires you to spin puns off your tongue like a standup comedienne? That's Sooz.

Another trademark of her life orientation was treating challenges with a strange but compelling combination of that levity and a talent for analytics. She seemed to register circumstances the way she easily found the high notes when performing; like there was some magical spell she'd received upon birth that helped her glide over whatever darkness the rest of us, particularly myself, were struggling to push through.

One chilly spring day, my boyfriend was out of town and Sooz and I were homesick for friends and family in Seattle. The boyfriend had left his old car—a Chrysler? (who knows—it was *old),* behind. "You can use it if you need it for an emergency," he'd cautioned. "But *only* for emergencies—like, if a hospital is required." Sooz and I, likely in that smoking room, ascertained that homesickness definitely qualified as an emergency, and that the old, rusty car could deliver us to the airport in Spokane, Washington, theoretically an hour and a half drive away.

We decided on a Thursday. The next morning, we quickly added a pack each of Marlboros to our overnight bags, located the key and walked the chilly three blocks to where the car was parked. I neglected to call my boyfriend and inform him of our plan.

The first hiccup was the discovery that the heating system wasn't working. It was around twenty degrees outside, so we (Sooz, cheerfully; me crankily) donned coats and gloves, only removing them to light cigarettes. The cigarette lighting was Sooz's job. I was hunched over the wheel, now in growing fear of my boyfriend's wrath and further perils ahead. Snow was predicted, and I'd never driven that car, let alone in snow. No heat wasn't fun, but a snowstorm would be catastrophic. And, as an Eeyore at heart, I expected the worst.

Twenty minutes out of town, disaster struck. The car suddenly lurched to the side and wouldn't drive straight. I pulled over to the side of the narrow highway, and we exited the car to ascertain what the issue might be. Flat tire.

I'd never changed a flat tire, nor had Sooz. There were no cell phones then, it was cold, and the cigarettes were now lighting one another non-stop. After about a half an hour, an angel disguised as a passing motorist stopped. He took pity on us and changed the tire. We cheered him on, shivering by the side of the road. He completed the task and we thanked him profusely, gratefully returning to our journey.

Snow was now imminent, and that car had never met a snow tire. Further, our angel had said something like the tires were all "as bald as an eagle" anyway. I was now terrified, but Sooz kept the conversation light, talking about how excited our parents would be when we surprised them, and what fun we'd have telling my boyfriend about our adventure. I figured, if that was so, maybe *she* could take the blame for our decision.

We slipped and slid a bit, but somehow stayed on the road, focused on the destination. Then, a half hour away from Spokane, the car locked up. To this day, I'm not sure what exactly happened, but it had to do with the brake system, or some kind of system. Bottom line, we could not move the car, and no angel motorist was going to change that.

My memory is foggy on the details, but the following happened, not necessarily in this order: we contacted the parents of some sorority sisters—strangers—and they agreed to pick us up, host us overnight, and somehow assist with getting the car off the road and into a shop; I called my boyfriend, who, for some reason, did not break up with me, and, most importantly, Sooz made the whole thing into an adventure.

I simply could not stay gloomy with her chirpy, "Isn't this a ball" reaction to the day's happenings. This, despite the fact that I owed my boyfriend a lot of money I didn't have for towing and repair of a car basically beyond repair, we had blackened our lungs aggressively that day, and spent the night in the first house I ever saw with plastic covering the living room furniture *and* the rugs.

Sooz found the whole thing hilarious, and as a result, I was forced to transform from an Eeyore to more of an agreeable Piglet. If I'd been with anyone else on that journey, I'm sure the story we'd retell decades later would read differently.

A few years later, on a very hot summer day, I was a bridesmaid in Sooz and Gordy's wedding. Standing behind the couple as they knelt for their vows, I fainted, making Gordy wonder if someone had written something suggestive on the heels of his shoes. Two other bridesmaids guided me backward and sat me on the front pew as the couple continued on, not sure what the rustling behind them might have been. *That* story has been told and retold countless times, again with good humor and laughter.

I can guarantee that, had the situation been reversed, I would *not* have been so generous with *my* laughter in the retelling. (Though, Sooz and Gordy *did* come late to my *second* wedding, so maybe there was a bit of payback).

More than a half century after the debacle of that car trip, Sooz is still the one to laugh first. I remain my wittiest in her company. And though

I am still an Eeyore at heart, whenever I'm with her, I invariably have the highest level of fun and leave infused with a dose of that lightness and laughter surrounding me like an invisible cloak—the remnants of which lasts for hours.

I always have a little talk with myself after being in Sooz's company, realizing how good it feels to lighten up and not take everything so seriously. "I *really* need to be more like Sooz," I have told myself for fifty years. Unfortunately, the magic within her has not transferred to me, but I am able, for some time, whenever I'm in her company, to deny my inner Eeyore.

No one else has been able to ignite that temporary transformation, and Sooz will always claim first prize, cosmically, for the accomplishment.

10

Mickey

Unexpected kindness is the most powerful, least costly, and most underrated agent of human change.

—Bob Kerrey

My friend Gail has never met a stranger. Never. Whether on an unfamiliar golf course or foreign shores, she assumes everyone is as happy as she to engage in conversation and learn about one another. Though I have fine social skills, I am the opposite of Gail. And at nineteen, I was not an open, trusting soul; a direct consequence of being raised to be wary of strangers and to expect danger and disaster as general protocol.

Not long after Sooz's and my disastrous adventure, I had a quarter abroad in Avignon, France. This is where Snow White had magically revealed the beauty of an orange, and where I began to hopscotch into a wider life experience; observing, maturing, and learning. Being exposed for the first time to a foreign culture (I have become forever a Francophile), studying and traveling in Southern France and living away from the constant verbal supervision of my mother and stepfather, I was allowed my first extended period of open-ended exploration. It was grand.

53

Once a week our group would board a bus and visit destinations focused on the art and history of the area. Every weekend night, we gathered for wine, cheese and bread and the rapturous conversation of youth. We were intellectually hungry, basking in the daily revelations of becoming citizens of the world.

One night, Jack, our French history instructor, invited me and John, a friend and "older" student at thirty-two, to the apartment of Jack's French girlfriend Suzanne. Apparently, the two had a once-a-year liaison that was re-activated every spring when Jack returned to teach. They were perhaps in their early forties, and I, sexually naïve, was transfixed by the sophistication of their casual, yet clearly passionate relationship. We drank wine and chatted; Suzanne with broken English and John and me with equally broken French. One of the lasting memories of my Avignon experience was listening to Jack, who spoke fluent French, translating Jacque Brel's signature song, "Ne Me Quitte Pas" from French to English in a voice nearly as melodious as the singer's.

I had joined the program believing that Laurie and I would spend the summer traveling together, but she had decided last minute not to go abroad, so, by the end of the quarter as our group began to venture out to various spots around the globe, I was all by myself.

Everything within me urged running back to the familiar, to get on an airplane and return to a safe and predictable existence in the States. Yet, in my heart, I did not want to go home. I yearned to be a free spirit like my fellow students as they began their travels with open enthusiasm. Still, my solitude and isolation were disheartening. Truly terrified but trying to be the person I wanted to be, I willed myself to stay in Europe and travel solo.

This was 1969, and *Europe on Five Dollars A Day* was the bible of young travelers. With that book, a Eurorail pass in my backpack, some money, and a determination to, despite my inner terror, venture out, I bid adieu to the hefty and good-willed French family that had hosted me for three months. I would miss their apricot jam on fresh croissants every morning and having a home to return to each night.

Once I began my terrifying adventure, I found it surprisingly easy to meet other travelers and pair up for few days, depending upon the destination. Sometimes I changed my itinerary just to have company. I was always careful with my selections, most often choosing females as my companions.

One exception was Joe, a sad and slightly goofy guy from Florida who I met on the train to Florence, and we joined forces for a few days. We were both *so* lonely; he was missing his girlfriend, I the security of my student group in Avignon, that we would, from the distance of twin beds in the cheap hotel rooms we found, fall asleep holding hands. I remember thinking how bold I was to travel with a strange boy, when in truth it was more like babysitting a much younger cousin. He was even less prepared for solo travel than I was.

I bought a switch blade and carved apples when I became uneasy with the looks from men on trains, believing that show of strength and panache surely protected me. What I really wanted during those lonely train rides and stays in hostels or dank hotel rooms was some fun, safe companions to get me through the summer, and not have to constantly monitor my safety margins. Finally, after a month of being alone, I met Matt and Bill, my mates for the rest of the season.

They were USC students and best friends, one student body president, the other student vice-president of the university, so I figured they were trustworthy. Smart fellows both, Matt had long hair and a beard while Bill was cleaner cut. This was just the beginning of the hippie movement world-wide, and, because of Matt's appearance, my new travel companions often received rude treatment from citizens, hotel and restaurant workers (beyond the usual French disdain). Americans overall were not a well-regarded group of travelers at that time, with Nixon at the helm and the stereotypical obnoxious American tourist in evidence wherever we went. I got used to hostile looks and comments about Matt (the gentlest soul one could imagine). I think Bill's short hair and my more traditional look saved us from any real unpleasantness.

On a stormy, rainy evening in Marseilles, our now established trio had taken our clothes to the laundromat. This was an infrequent occurrence, that night necessitated by the weather and the unspoken understanding that laundry day was, in every way, overdue. The wait for machines was interminable, and we had skipped dinner to try to find a time when the washers would be more accessible. The rain continued, beating against the windows, generating dampness that permeated the interior of the laundromat. After two hours of waiting for a machine, we were cold, hungry, and cranky. Then, as a washer became available, and bracing ourselves for several more hours onsite to claim a dryer once our clothes were clean, an attractive woman in her thirties began a conversation with us.

Mickey did not speak English and I was the only one in our trio with a small offering of French, but she seemed very eager to learn about us and our travels. Another hour passed; our clothes having graduated from the wash but with no post-graduate possibility as no dryers were available.

We resignedly started packing our damp clothes into our backpacks, hypothesizing glumly that stringing them across our hostel room would be of some help in the drying overnight. We weren't hopeful, but it was clear that a French drying experience was not in our near future. Still chatting with Mickey, we were surprised when she invited us to her apartment to use her home dryer and enjoy a light respite. She didn't hesitate in her invitation due to Matt's appearance, and the two boys quickly agreed.

I was wary. She *seemed* nice, but why would she invite three bedraggled strangers, one of whom looked *slightly* like an ax murderer, into her home? I could hear my mother's voice in my head. "Do NOT go to that woman's house. Who knows what might happen?" I really didn't want to accept the invitation but was outvoted. Loading our packs, heavier than when we'd begun the adventure because of their dampness, we followed her to her apartment a few blocks away.

She seemed excited to be in our company. We learned she was divorced and had a child with cerebral palsy who lived in an institution.

Shyly showing us pictures of the girl, explaining the extent of her disability and her own inability to care for the girl, the sorrow she transmitted while explaining the situation was palpable, and the mixture of regret and grief about her circumstances somehow, in those few hours, brought the four of us into a circle of empathy and intimacy. Retrospectively, I understood how lonely she must have been—how horribly sad; single and away from her beloved child. Then, I was focused on the generosity of a stranger.

She concocted a modest feast with the inevitable table wine, as gracious as if we'd been extended an invitation the week before. As the dryer hummed with the weight of our clothes, Mickey put French music on her record player and detailed the tunes she was sharing. She couldn't believe we didn't know her compatriot, the famous singer Johnny Holiday. Several hours later, we departed, folded and dry laundry in our bags and a new friend in our hearts. We'd had a glimpse into the personal life of a friendly French citizen, enough older than us in age and life experience that the exchange felt more genuine, more heartfelt than those we had with international students in our travels. It was as if Mickey's personal tragedy, paired with her open friendliness, was its own chapter in a singular book we'd been gifted, and we were the privileged readers.

I had taken her contact information, meaning to send her some American music upon my return to the U.S., but lost it, and felt badly about my lack of follow through. I've spent some time in the decades since trying to locate her with no luck. Yet, the kindness she showed us that evening changed how I viewed future interactions with strangers from other cultures. When my mother's inner voice, like Jiminy Cricket in a very bad mood, would caution me away from the horrible people and things they might do to me, I remembered Mickey. I became more open to the unfamiliar.

Ironically, shortly after returning home from France, I overheard a fellow in a Rite Aid with a French accent trying to understand the clerk's directives about payment. I might not have intervened before meeting Mickey, but instead jumped in and awkwardly translated. I befriended the fellow, Jean, who turned out to be a member of Jacque Cousteau's crew. We had many interactions in the following months while the company furloughed in Seattle, including me taking Jean to my mother and stepfather's house for dinner, where he thoroughly charmed them. "See?" I wanted to say. "See what happens when you trust?"

So long ago, Mickey opened a door that I had been taught was locked—one to approach with distrust. The consequent broadening of my mind and heart would likely have occurred regardless as I matured, but I've always felt it would have taken much longer to discover the riches I found in the opening if not for Mickey.

Mickey wasn't a "friend" in the traditional sense, but her act of friendliness captured the essence and meaning of the word; kindness, trust, and open giving of self. I gratefully include her in the collection of women who helped to form me.

11

Carolina

It has always fascinated me that we're prepared to end a romantic relationship that is no longer working but are generally reluctant to do the same with friendships. Not all friendships are meant to last for life. People evolve, and friendships evolve with them.

—Sarah Morgan, *Family for Beginners*

Occasionally, you meet someone who was meant to be in your life for a reason, but not forever. Carolina was one of those people for me.

Thus far in my sheltered existence, I hadn't yet had a friend who pushed me outside my comfort zone. Then, I met Carolina. Now, there was someone who challenged me to try new, previously self-forbidden experiences. All the years I knew her, I felt like she was escorting me to the front seat of a roller coaster. (As a point of reference, to this day I've never set foot on a roller coaster. But that's not Carolina's fault.)

When Laurie and I were juniors in high school, we began dating boys from Seattle. We had a good friend, a guy who'd transferred to a private school there, and he introduced us to several of his buddies. We began to go to dances—our weekend activity in those days—with those Seattle boys.

At one of the dances we met Carolina. She was friendly and striking. Most of the private school girls weren't particularly friendly to Laurie and me, not being happy their boy zone was being invaded by outsiders. Carolina, though, also attending a public school in the area, was always welcoming, and for the next couple of years the three of us often talked, comparing school experiences or boyfriend status. The three of us then became part of a coagulated group that spent most of the halcyon days before leaving for college at a summer home belonging to my boyfriend's family. We had that last summer of our youth reveling in the ripeness of the time and the seemingly endless possibilities for our future.

While Laurie and I, middling students, went to a state university, Carolina, very bright, headed to UCLA. She began writing me letters, which one did in those days. I remember sitting in a small room in the sorority with Laurie, opening an envelope from Carolina that contained a single balloon but no letter.

"She sent a balloon?" said Laurie. "What are you supposed to do with it?"

"I don't know," I said, peering closely at the thing. Then I saw ink marks on the surface. "Maybe blow it up?"

I did so, and, once I tied off the balloon, found a letter Carolina had written on its surface. She'd gone to the trouble of blowing the thing up, tying it off, writing a letter on its surface, then letting the air out. I thought that was about the most brilliant thing I'd ever seen. (Remember, I was the middling student.)

After I returned from France, I transferred to the University of Washington, and Carolina transferred north to Washington from UCLA. We rented the top floor of a house together, and there began a friendship markedly different than those I'd had before.

Carolina was not only extremely bright, but she was, and I mean this in the best possible way, a little bit crazy. Remember Katie, the Can-Can girl from Chapter Two? Carolina was the grownup version. Plus... more.

Laurie and I were good girls, and nice girls. Carolina was also, but she had a wildness to her, an openness to new experiences and the changes

60

in the current culture that were an anathema to my mindset. I wanted to be open to behaviors emblematic of the times like marching against the Vietnam war or even experimenting with drugs, but that wasn't how I'd been coached my whole life. Neither had Carolina, but that did not stop her.

By now, most of us, even me, smoked weed—we called it dope at that time—on a regular basis. Carolina could do this nightly, carry a class load of eighteen hours, and get straight A's. I tried to follow her lead, but instead struggled, dropping courses, and, with the exception of English, barely passed most of my classes. I aspired to be as academically talented as she was, but I simply didn't have the goods. While Carolina could study efficiently for two hours for her heavy class load and be successful, my inferior academic prowess, paired with the idea that studying a *half* hour a night would be sufficient, doomed me to full mediocre status.

Carolina didn't care that I couldn't match her report card success. What she really wanted was for me to loosen up on all fronts. That included joining her in trying other drugs besides weed, specifically acid and mescaline. I was adamant I would never try anything stronger than marijuana, but she continued to try to persuade me to open the door to consciousness via chemicals. This was, by the way, the same girl who always ridiculed me for having the mindset of an eighty-year-old in the body of a twenty-year-old.

One night, around three in the morning, I woke up to find Carolina sitting on the floor of my bedroom.

"Rom," she whispered. "You just have to try mescaline. It will change your life—I promise. Try it *now.*" She spent an hour arguing her case, explaining in minute detail what she was seeing in my dark bedroom that, apparently for her, was filled with colorful, live-action-wonders, then fell asleep on the floor next to my bed.

I never veered from my resolve, but Carolina's descriptions of her occasional dips into more serious indulgences informed me about what many college students our age were trying, believing in, and experimenting with, resulting in a dramatic infusion of change in the culture of the country. It was like having a travel guide into a whole new world, except I didn't have to get on the airplane. (By now, you can imagine I hate flying.) I could see things through Carolina's eyes. Her descriptions and tales of a craziness far exceeding my universe, intrigued, but also terrified me.

But the best part of Carolina wasn't the ongoing challenge of changing my basic personality. It was the laughing. Laurie and I laughed often, but it wasn't because of our brilliance. Rather, it was the shared years and references, as it is with many friendships, that formed the basis of our mirth. But Carolina, with her quick wit, bawdy sense of humor and ability to somehow be simultaneously shocking and thrilling, delivered a brand of hilarity I'd never known.

She had a red convertible sports car, and one summer day she was smoking a joint while driving down the freeway, me in the passenger seat. I wasn't happy she was combining those two activities, but somehow Carolina always got away with bad behavior in my presence, despite my resolve to not succumb to her influence. Suddenly, she dropped the joint in her lap.

"Quick," she shrieked, "get it, GET it!" She lifted her rear end five inches from the seat, steering with one hand as I grappled for the slender, smoking item.

"I can't reach it," I yelled, wind in our ears, the speed of the car not assisting the rescue.

The peril of the moment, the car now weaving, Carolina's body pretzeled backward, and the ridiculousness of the situation hit us both, and shrieks of laughter carried us down the freeway. I'd never felt such pure abandon. In that one instant I was released from my standard fear of— let's face it—everything. That moment of succumbing to whatever was happening, whether my choice or not, was not how I lived in the world. But there I was, right where Carolina had placed me.

She finally made a quick exit and pulled over, retrieving the joint and taking a long toke once we controlled ourselves. I *never* would have smoked dope while driving, couldn't afford or had the style for a red convertible, and generally avoided any activity my mother wouldn't have sanctioned. But my companion was a rebel—someone who didn't so much think outside of the box as create a whole other way of perceiving what a box might be.

Carolina exposed me to another, completely different kind of female; one who didn't follow rules but could rule whatever she pleased, reveled in elevating situations to peak conditions, always pushing the envelope, while antithetically camouflaging a thoughtful, surprisingly sensitive soul. We luckily survived that foolish freeway drive, but I never permitted a repeat of such risky behavior with her at the wheel.

We ended up sharing a couple different living situations after college. By our late twenties, I'd married, with Carolina as my maid of honor. She remained single the rest of her life.

When I was a young mother, working full time and with two children under four, Carolina, now two states away, would call me for a long conversation as had been our practice during our years of friendship. Those chats typically ran around an hour, as she always had stories to tell. She had no idea of the challenges I faced in sustaining a grown-up conversation. I was a mom; she was still dating. I had no free time; her time was her own. And, her favorite topic of conversation during those calls was *always* every sordid detail of her latest dating/sex disaster.

No one could tell a story like Carolina, but my children didn't know that, or care. Those calls were my only source for her unique brand of humor every month, a distinctly different kind of entertainment than the antics of two darling children, and I was loath to give them up.

"Mommy will give you candy if you play with the things in the cupboard," I would whisper to the four-year-old who only got candy on Halloween and Christmas. "Here," I would say, offering the two-year-old a bowl of water and various cups while Carolina described the sexual predilections of the radio host she'd temporarily beguiled, "You can pour water anywhere you want on the floor."

Despite those delicious and normally forbidden opportunities, my children ardently resented those conversations. "Her again?" my daughter would say, and though I felt guilty neglecting her and her brother during that hour, I couldn't resist the calls.

The stories—oh, the stories—I would hear from Carolina about single life in her thirties, then forties. They were deliciously wicked, irreverent, and unlike any other adventures I heard about from any other female. I didn't want to live that life, didn't envy it a bit, but listening to her was like being back on that freeway in that giddy, heady delight and surrender.

Carolina is now in the same clique as Deb and Gabby. We had, after over forty years of friendship, an unrepairable rift. I had to let her go, and I did so with no regrets. Yet, again, where I am in my life now, and wherever she is, it doesn't stain the imprint she had on me.

Because of her, I have been open to other wild spirits in my life. I've always learned from them and consistently laughed with them at a deeper and higher level than with other, more stable friends. The rule-obeying, "good girl" still finds a distinct brand of giddiness and freedom in the company of those women. And, I can spot them a mile away. It's always a treat to find such creatures and spend time in their company, but they are not a steady diet. Too rich; too unbalanced. Yet, I find a singular kind of joy in knowing them, thanks to Carolina.

There are moments when I'm driving that same stretch of highway Carolina and I covered that day in her red convertible when I recall our hysterical laughter, the unfamiliar abandon within me. I'll shake my head and chuckle, remembering. The free spirit, the wild girl, the experimenter and bold explorer, loosened, in the years I knew her, the fabric of my tightly woven psyche, and, consequently, memorably expanded my universe.

12

Revka

CONSCIOUSNESS RAISING

Water and a bubble on it are one and the same. The bubble has its birth in the water, floats on it, and is ultimately resolved into it. Likewise, your consciousness is born in your brain, goes through various states in your lifetime and ultimately resolves into the brain.

—Abhijit Naskar, *Autobiography of God: Biopsy of A Cognitive Reality*

The same boyfriend whose car I'd misused on the adventure near Spokane went out of my life for a few years. Then, when I was twenty-one, we reconnected and I, living in Seattle at the time, decided to move to the Bay area in California to start a life, or at least *have* a life, with JJ.

JJ was a charismatic, fun-loving guy. His father had died young, but I'd met and adored his mother and older sister. In turn, my mother was more charmed by JJ than anyone I'd brought home as a boyfriend. That was a potent sanction for me, and though my parents weren't thrilled I would be living with JJ, I think they could see we were not ready for marriage. It never even entered the conversation.

This was 1970, and "hippies" were just beginning their evolution in San Francisco, the incubator for so many changes in the culture of the country. I didn't know anyone who looked or behaved like the legions of young people I saw in colorful garb, long, untamed hair and vacant, blissful smiles on their faces. I remember walking through Golden Gate Park and feeling like I had somehow been transported into another space, another time (a result of something the people inhabiting the park were doing with drugs). In Europe, I'd been exposed to various cultures, but they were based on centuries of traditions, different customs and languages. Even my friend Matt, whom I traveled with in Europe and looked like those kids in the park, didn't match the profile as he was, to my mind, academically and socially credentialled. As an extremely uptight and constantly worried person, I found myself thinking, as I watched the spaced-out masses, "But, how will you get a job?" and "What do your parents think—are they worried about you?"

JJ, however, was completely comfortable with people who, if coming face-to-face with such creatures, would have caused the color to leave the faces of my mother and stepfather. I understood immediately that this was to be part of our life together—interacting with this whole new breed of American. I worried that I wouldn't find common ground with his friends, or, more importantly, that they would reject me because I was so straight and rigid in my outlook and experience.

Not long after we'd settled into the top floor of a little duplex in Hayward, California, JJ began talking about David and Revka.

JJ had met David on a city bus; David a driver, JJ a passenger. Because JJ was a very outgoing guy, he often had exchanges with strangers, and somehow the hippie driving the bus and the much straighter looking fellow riding it became friends. JJ had visited the commune where David lived with several others of his ilk, and one night, JJ told me he was taking me to meet them all.

I was extremely apprehensive. At that time, though I'd smoked marijuana with Carolina, it really wasn't something I was inclined to do on a regular basis, and wasn't that what hippies did all the time? More importantly, I was, despite the fact that I'd left Seattle and the zone of my parents, still a puppet to their expectations. The first priority in the home of my mother and stepfather was appearance. The first order of their comments, whenever I crossed the threshold of their doorstep, was always an analysis of my clothing and hair. Their observations of others inevitably included a similar breakdown of their appearance. I felt, by crossing such a symbolic and literal societal threshold—an actual commune with real hippies—as if my parents could somehow intuit, thousands of miles away, the crime I would be committing by socializing with the visually unacceptable.

The commune was, in classic San Francisco style, situated on a steep hill. The apartment had three or four bedrooms and one bathroom. I never knew how many people actually lived in each room. The ambiance was pretty much what I'd imagined; messy, signs on the fridge saying whose food was whose, and all sorts of Indian bedspreads covering the furniture. The most notable lifestyle statement was in the bathroom. When I went to use it, I discovered the inhabitants didn't believe in toilet paper, at least as a regular practice. Every person had their own rag, presumably for urination cleanup. I don't know quite how that accomplished everything that needed to be done in that room, but I'll never forget learning about the practice and thinking, "Boy, these are *real* hippies!"

Revka was the first person I met that day. As we walked in, she was sitting on a couch, reading a book, and looked up with a beatific, welcoming smile. A native New Yorker, she had the accent, plus an exotic, ethnic appearance. Her parents were, as I recall, from Egypt and Israel, and she didn't look like anyone I'd ever met in monochromatic Washington state. I remember studying her face, so distinct and striking, and envying just how *interesting* she looked. If you'd lined us up next to one another, I was bland, she was spicy. I had straight, long brown hair; her hair was equally long but so curly every single tendril seemed to have had a mind of its own. Compared to Revka, I was a flat paper doll, while she was three dimensional. She was heavy breasted and slightly plump for our age group, and was passionate about Greenpeace, liberal causes and the political climate of the country. I'd heard of Greenpeace but didn't have any curiosity about its mission and knew absolutely nothing about politics.

And that was it; Revka was the first woman I met my age who had a well-developed social consciousness. The girlfriends I'd had until then cared about and prioritized the same thing I did; how to find and nurture the perfect relationship. That was followed by a *slight* interest in making money, but that was just practicality, not ambition. I knew I had to pay bills, but that was something I would do in support of whatever long-term relationship I would finalize in the near future.

Revka didn't talk about the fact that she was or wasn't in a relationship. She was interested in having one but cared more about ideas and what her career path would be. She was ambitious in her professional aspirations. She also owned her unusual appearance and didn't obsess about the few extra pounds or try to tame her hair to look like everyone else. With an awareness of global issues, a searing intellectual curiosity, and a commitment to taking care of the earth and all its creatures, Revka was not just unique in my experience; she was to be another revelation. Not like learning how to adjust expectations and honor circumstances like when Diana became pregnant, but to be in the presence of a peer who prioritized global issues above personal life, principles above superficiality.

Despite my initial reservations, I was immediately drawn to her and David, and they were gracious in their acceptance of JJ's uptight, rigid girlfriend. We spent a fair amount of time in one another's houses; JJ and I joining in the potlucks at the commune and David and Revka crossing the bridge to our little duplex in Hayward for soup and bread, our primary sustenance in those days. Each time I would see her, Revka would talk about a new book she was reading or share her thoughts about a recent international incident. She was always current on what was happening in the burgeoning environmental movement. The contrast to my life was subtle but instructive. When we'd meet, she added layers of meaning to the conversation, never judging my lack of contribution nor proselytizing, just setting an example. Though we were the same age, it felt a bit like I was a gawky teenager and she the nice teacher who didn't mind hanging out with her student.

Revka went on to volunteer for Greenpeace, return to New York to get advanced degrees in gifted education and have a long career as a professor at a prestigious university on the East coast. We stayed in touch for a couple of decades. I connected her with Carolina at one point, and they became good friends, their single and independent lives more aligned.

I haven't seen Revka in more than thirty years, but her impact on how I would aspire to something beyond myself is evident. Though I didn't follow her example when it came to prioritizing relationship issues, I *did* now have an understanding of the importance of viewing the planet and its challenges on a broader, more humanitarian scale. That was a big leap for me.

Not immediately, but still in my early twenties, I made my first contribution to a cause, mailing checks to Greenpeace, feeling a little thrill of sanctimony at my offering. That's an important step in becoming a grownup; the awareness of ones' place in the larger picture. I also began looking at global issues as something that wasn't just for hippies. This was *my* earth too, and I could have a voice in its future. My voice was more like a whisper, but it was a beginning. Now, of course, my understanding of those same concerns is at a peak, and my commitment to the concerns Revka had fifty years ago is substantial. I wish I'd been able to have increased my awareness sooner. Yet, knowing Revka, actually understanding that a young woman could live with such passion and commitment to a cause beyond herself, impacted my emotional and intellectual development. I didn't change dramatically, but change began, and might not have without her steadfast example.

13

Erika

TIME TO GROW UP

Bad advice will blind you, good advice will instruct you, excellent advice will enlighten you, and transcendent advice will elevate you.

—Matshona Dhliwayo

Influences upon character or behavior are often predictable. Sometimes, they're unexpected. For most of us, the power of influence comes from a conglomeration of media, literature, friends and family. Importantly, sometimes it's the right person at the right time saying the right words that delivers the greatest impact.

My living arrangement with JJ lasted around a year but didn't have the weight of the future in it. After not much discussion and with full agreement, I bade him good-bye with fondness and appreciation for our shared experience. I packed up my Ford Fairlane 500, my cat, and a young woman from Revka's commune who was looking for an adventure, and headed toward the Northwest.

After a very long day of driving with an unhappy cat who didn't find the litter box placement behind the driver's seat quite to his specifications, plus trying to carry on a conversation with a girl I didn't know and who, unfortunately, was at the opposite end of the spectrum from

Revka in terms of intellectual capacity, we finally arrived back in Seattle. I dropped the girl off in the middle of the night at what I assumed was the Northwest version of a commune. Before I found an apartment and job, I bunked at my mother and stepfather's house for a few weeks. There, Erika was waiting with her opinions.

Erika was my mother's Latvian cleaning lady, but that hardly describes who she was in my life, and, I believe, my mother's. Once a week, for eight hours every Friday, Erika, who was, as my stepfather used to say, a "sturdy" woman, would knock on the front door, enter the house with a gruff yet professional greeting and begin her chores. She had an open, Slavic face, with large, sea glass blue eyes. Her white/blond hair was always beautifully coiffed, and she usually wore skirts with tights, so the final effect was an interesting combination of practicality and an aspiration for glamour. She worked all morning; dusting, scouring bathrooms, scrubbing the kitchen floor on her hands and knees, then taking a full hour for lunch, always sharing the kitchen table with my mother. The afternoon was for lighter duties like ironing and vacuuming. Friday after Friday after Friday for at least ten years, Erika would arrive promptly at eight a.m. and leave at five p.m. As far as I know, she never missed a week. My mother also had her hair done on Fridays, but never during lunch, because that was when she, and I, as often as possible, would be the recipient of the delight that was Erika.

In those days, both my mother and I smoked cigarettes. Erika did not, but she tolerated the smelly and messy byproduct as we sat around my mother's kitchen table and chatted. But before we got out the ashtray, we spent most of the lunch hour listening to Erika. My mother would make the three of us grilled cheese sandwiches and chocolate cokes, and we'd *talk*.

The conversation was largely filled with Erika's recounting her life in Latvia, her husband Arnie's many faults and her children's countless, wayward choices. There wasn't an opinion Erika had, on any number of subjects, that spent any time inside her mind before she would declare, loudly, and with certainty, her final edict. Politics, clothing selection, the right size of diamonds (she was fascinated by diamonds), television shows—it didn't matter; Erika had the final say.

And she should have, because she was brilliant, witty in an old-world way, and very astute about people's strengths and weaknesses. I'm sure she'd found the hidden vodka bottles and glasses that I had located for years in my mother and stepfather's home, and understood, as did I, the price my mother paid for living with an alcoholic. But on that subject, Erika never said a word.

She and my mother were very fond of one another, and Erika brought an earthiness to that home that none of the women in my parent's social group could have offered, even if they'd wanted. My mother had grown up poor but was now very comfortable. Erika grew up during the war years in Latvia and had started a new life with Arnie, and her perspective brought the most authentic conversations I ever heard into that kitchen.

Once I found an apartment and a job working nights, and for several years after my return from California, I would arrive on Friday mornings with a full load of dirty laundry, a fresh pack of cigarettes, and gleeful anticipation of lunch with Erika. She not only enlivened my mother's socially oppressed life, (there was only one star of the show in that household, and it was not my mother), but Erika also grounded me.

I was flailing, understanding that waitressing wasn't a long-term career option, but not knowing what I wanted to do. At this point, after my mother had informed me that my three choices were teacher, secretary or nurse, I was trying to select just one (puppet that I was). Erika had no patience for my indecision. And she had *less* patience for the holdover dress code I had adopted after spending time with Revka and being exposed to the more relaxed garb of the San Francisco area. I was what one friend called a "pseudo hippie"; I tried to dress the part, feeling edgy, yet glamorous, without doing all the drugs. To me, going bra-less, wearing my long hair in braids with a hairband encircling my forehead and accenting torn jeans with a tie-dyed t-shirt made me look absolutely fabulous, timeless, and impressive.

My mother had her opinion about my looks. She always had—but somehow, it was Erika's pronouncements, and one in particular, that shifted my outlook about my appearance.

I had been trying to set up interviews with graduate schools—something that was *barely* within my reach—and pictured the impression I'd make with the interviewers; a hip, ready to learn-future-leader-of-tomorrow-in-a laid-back-sort-of-way. Erika, ever astute, somehow intuited my plan. She took what I could only describe as a meaty fist and banged it on the table several times. She then hissed/yelled "Romney, if you don't take those goddamn jeans off, put on a bra and a skirt and some nylons, you'll never get anywhere." She then proceeded to delineate what a hapless offering I *really* was.

Because she was Erika and not my mother, and particularly because I knew Erika loved me in her way, I listened. If my mother had said the same thing, without the pounding on the table, I would have rejected the opinion, staying firm in my grandiose perception of my hip persona. But it was Erika. I listened. And in a moment, I grew up in one small quadrant. It was like I had been poised for graduation but hadn't completed the last course because it was just a little too hard. Ultimately, we all have to finish that last course, and if we're lucky, there's an Erika to push us through.

I swallowed the picture of the hipster from California, retrieved some nylons from the back of my mother's drawer, pulled my long hair back into a demure ponytail, and interviewed at three universities. The fact that I didn't get into my top choice was due to my lackluster academic skills, not my visual presentation.

Often, in the years following my adjustment in my appearance, when I would prepare for a job interview, I'd think about how Erika would advise me to dress. That framing device was always very effective, except for the time I put a Tampax in my front jacket pocket to transfer into my purse before leaving the house but forgot. The noticeable white cylinder sat upright and evident throughout the interview. I didn't get that job, and I certainly never told Erika.

14

Fran

A TABLE IS MORE THAN A TABLE

Delaying gratification is a process of scheduling the pain and pleasure of life in such a way as to enhance the pleasure by meeting and experiencing the pain first and getting it over with. It is the only decent way to live.

—M. Scott Peck

I grew up in two different households; my father's in my early childhood and my stepfather's after the age of thirteen, but in neither did I accrue an awareness about money, saving, budgets or planning. This was, apparently, the territory of grownups, particularly males. Though I'd put myself through graduate school, I never balanced a checkbook nor did I hesitate to put something I wanted, rather than needed, that was outside my bank reserves, on a credit card.

My first real lesson in finance, one that I was finally was able to apply into my thinking, came from my friend Fran.

Not long after Erika helped to change the trajectory of my life, I attended graduate school, met my first husband, and began a career in education. My husband, who'd grown up in less secure financial circumstances than I, also had no clue about money.

In our second year of marriage, I unexpectedly became pregnant with our first child. It was a bit of an adjustment after a lofty plan for two doctorates and careers that we felt would change the face of education, but we quickly adjusted to our new reality. My husband later earned his advanced degrees, but after having our daughter, then a son, I reversed my priorities. Family first, possible career advancement later. Maybe.

I found myself in an unfamiliar world, as all new parents do. It wasn't the baby minding, nursing and nurturing I found puzzling; it was everything else you had to do at the same time. I'd never been an organized person on any front, whether it was with lesson plans or planning meals, and my husband didn't cook, so I was left to untangle the multiple and labyrinthian tasks of house management, child management and teaching duties.

In my first teaching job as a special education instructor, I met a fellow teacher, Fran, also married to another educator (my husband was a school psychologist). We were all friendly but became more so when we both had become pregnant around the same time and then ended up together in our first Lamaze class. Sitting in a room with other couples and discussing the A, B, C's of basic body functions is a real bonding experience.

Then, our two daughters were born within two weeks of one another, and both, we discovered early on, would share the same name. After our daughters' births, Fran and I spent a lot of time together, each with our babies, thrilled to be sharing the delights and challenges of new motherhood. Our second children arrived two years later, again two weeks apart.

That was what Fran and I had in common; our burgeoning motherhood. Everything else? Diametrically opposed. Fran had the cleanest house of anyone I've ever known besides my beloved mother-in-law, and that title never changed in all the years she was an at-home parent, eventually of three children. While I had been fired by a cleaning lady we couldn't afford once I had my second child, ("Mrs. G, I simply cannot function in a home where the mother does not dispose of dirty diapers properly"), Fran somehow disinfected her household with every diaper change, whistling like a bluebird from a Walt Disney film, with nary a diaper, or scent of a diaper to be found. I barely put food on the table at every meal; Fran had her menus planned *a month* in advance. My laundry tasks averaged weeks behind schedule with piles not based on color, but the level of exhaustion I was feeling when I threw them in the general direction of the washing machine. Fran's laundry room was so empty and sparkling, it always seemed like I heard a little self-satisfied chuckle whenever I looked in, hoping to sight a spare pair of dirty underwear caught behind a door.

This efficiency always impressed me, but it wasn't what changed my life perspective.

Fran and her husband moved away from our area of the state when their children were school-aged, and consequently, in the next decade or so, we saw one another infrequently. When they bought a brand-new house, though, I brought my kids down to visit for the day. Fran gave me a tour of what was, of course, an immaculate home, one that nearly tripled the square footage of their first starter house.

When we came to the dining room, it was empty.

"Didn't you have a dining room table?" I asked.

"There was no dining room at the old house—remember? We just had that little table in the kitchen."

"When's it coming?" I asked, surveying the room bereft of even a chair.

"We're saving," she answered.

Time passed, with communication via Christmas cards and occasional phone calls. Once again, anxious for a catch up, I toted my kids a couple of hours down the freeway for a visit with Fran and her family. All our children were bigger, of course, but happy to reconnect. As we sat in her family room chatting about our current lives, I noted the dining room was still empty.

"Are you *still* saving for a table?" I asked, thoughtlessly.

"We have a certain one in mind," Fran said.

"Why don't you just buy a cheap one in the meantime?" I offered.

"There's one we're saving for," she answered.

Both of our families were struggling with money. I had gone back to work and Fran remained at home, plus had added one more child, so their economic situation was more challenging. But the bottom line was, neither family was flourishing financially. Money was tight, and it felt like the demands always exceeded the reserves.

At our house, if there was an item, we couldn't afford that we wanted, we charged it. We had absolutely no money sense, nor sensibility. We simply didn't know better. But Fran and her husband Jan, from the on-set of their marriage, had a budget, a plan, and a disciplined execution.

The differences between the two families had been evident for some time. Fran and Jan had one car they shared during their first few years of marriage; we'd had two, both bought on time. We bought a dining room table at Goodwill, still one we really couldn't afford, because we couldn't imagine going without. Fran and Jan did not. We were always behind on bills and never able to have an honest conversation about establishing a budget and implementing it responsibly. It bothered me greatly, but it was the pattern we'd established, while our friends somehow organized and implemented a plan to manage their money.

Fran and her husband didn't buy that dining room table for quite a while. The room remained empty, the family eating in the kitchen, happily, and debt-free.

I realized much later what an indicator that level of commitment and sacrifice meant; not about financial management, but specifically about how a good marriage works. The empty dining room at Fran's house came to symbolize not a lack, but a richness I learned to envy. Recall-ing that missing table served as a reminder about what really matters; not things, but commitment to values; not immediate gratification, but communication and sacrifice.

I wasn't able to apply those lessons for many years, but, thanks to Fran's example, I learned to look beyond choices in life and to examine their motivation and meaning, adjusting the balance between want and need. It was one of many takeaways she provided over decades of friendship. Another is the joy of hearing her astounding belly laugh, but that's a different story.

15

Sharon

I've always liked quiet people. You never know if they're dancing in a daydream or if they're carrying the weight of the world.

—John Green

A round the same time Fran and I were cleaning, or, in my case, not cleaning, our homes, I met Sharon. She was also an educator, a speech therapist, and I worked closely with her as I started the very first special education class in our elementary school.

Initially, it struck me as ironic that she was a speech therapist, because she was *very* quiet and shy. This wasn't an issue in her work with the students but was evident whenever speaking with her or in observing her interactions in the teacher's room. There, she'd usually sit silently, often a bit out of reach, responding to any query but not initiating conversations. Most teachers, by nature, have to be outgoing, with a lot of social energy.

Sharon was unusual compared to the rest of us. Though she was constantly in and out of classrooms, when she'd enter and remove a child for their therapy it was as if a butterfly had fluttered in and somehow magically transported the human weight of a seven-year-old to another location. Her presence, as you can imagine, was very calming for the children. But whenever I tried to have a conversation that didn't involve our shared students, I had to work hard to draw her out or speak at length. I knew she was shy but hadn't figured out how to break through that social barrier. Drawn to her gentle presence, I kept looking for a way to connect.

Sharon had her first child before I did, and when her daughter was nine months old, Sharon mentioned that her mother-in-law was coming to visit. She seemed, in her subdued way, to be in a bit of a panic about the state of her housekeeping. She was working full time and perhaps experiencing a bit of the challenge I would face in another year; how to manage it all. I had the sense that she might be a casual housekeeper like myself. Turns out she wasn't; she was just an overworked professional with a child at home and the upcoming visit from a relative was a stressful situation.

I somewhat aggressively invited myself over to help spiff up the house and impress her husband's mother. I hoped we'd be more comfortable around one another outside of school. That opening was the beginning of our friendship. The cleaning was the perfect ice breaker; we didn't have to talk much, her daughter was very entertaining, and the shared tasks did its job of making us more comfortable outside of our professional environment.

We began spending time together, including later with our children, gathering in parks and in one another's homes, enjoying watching our kids' interactions. I was usually the initiator, but Sharon seemed to enjoy our shared interests.

She was a wonderful model of a calm and loving parent, providing her kids, all of them brilliant, with tremendous creative and open-ended learning experiences. While I tended, in perfect teacher mode, to constantly provide my children with more structured opportunities outside of school, Sharon's home was a very different environment; more open, yet with stimulating materials the children could manipulate themselves. That inspired me to try different activities and opportunities for my own kids.

Again, like Fran, when her kids were school-aged, Sharon moved out of the area. Whenever I could, I would visit her in her new home a couple of hours away. Some of my fondest memories of our times together were when our children were outside playing. We would sit in her sunny kitchen, drinking strong tea with fresh cream from a local dairy and eating just-baked pastries.

It seemed so European and indulgent to have *both* cream and pastries, but it was part of the treat of spending time with Sharon. It felt like I'd been invited into a small and secret club for special spirits who would speak softly and thoughtfully as a matter of course. The best of it was listening to Sharon's carefully offered thoughts about parenting, marriage and the issues in our personal and professional lives.

Spending time with her was a very different experience than with other mothers; the pace was not free flowing, the laughter sometimes more halting. It was such a notable change, I found myself trying to entertain her, to speed up the back and forth, to have Sharon adjust to *my* way of communicating rather than stepping back and falling into her rhythm. Finally, over the years, I learned to relax into her pace rather than expecting Sharon to adjust to my much more frenetic style.

That was, and is, the gift of Sharon. She's like a Zen master, and she has been a great life teacher for me. Her presence requires patience, and I have never been a patient person. Every time I am with her, I am reminded of the importance of breathing, of paying attention, of not focusing on what *I* want to say, but on what she has to offer. That mindset of coming from quiet is one I should practice more, but it's ironically easiest when I am with Sharon.

We've now known one another for well over forty years. She is still very quiet, and I assume, shy. In the decades we've been friends, I've never asked her if she thought she *was* shy, just as she's never asked me why I always speak so quickly and bluntly. There is always a short period of time before a flow arrives in our conversation, and sometimes it doesn't come as quickly as impatient me would like it to. I've learned, over the years, to let Sharon set the pace, unfold her contributions, not needing a standard or typical rhythm, but to let the silences rest comfortably, and with trust.

Invariably, our time together is filled with discussions about the important things. Not just our children or grandchildren, but how we feel about family on the deepest level. Whenever I have a real concern about my kids, it's Sharon I will turn to for advice or solace. Her wisdom and measured responses to my impulsive and overly emotional reactions calm me and guide me toward a more grounded reality.

She sets an example in other ways. A model citizen of her community, she drives medical patients off the island where she lives and into Seattle, spending whole days caring for strangers. She and her husband have a magical garden, and birdwatching has led to a leadership role in the Audubon Society.

In my treasured circle of close friends, some are "noisier" than others. All bring something different into my life. But Sharon remains like that silent butterfly who transported, a child at a time, those small souls out of my classroom. They always returned a little bit wiser, calmer, and with skills and insights about themselves that no one else provided. As have I.

16

Priscilla

A Legacy of Love

Anyone who does anything to help a child is a hero to me.

—Fred Rogers

I met Priscilla when I was in graduate school and was a TA for her husband, Max, in the Special Education department at Western Washington University in Bellingham, Washington. Max and Priscilla were twenty years older than me, and had five children, a couple of them near my age. Over the two years I studied and worked in the department, they welcomed my family into their home often, along with other faculty. At those gatherings, I always found myself seeking out Priscilla's company.

Max presented as a kind-hearted, professorial type. Priscilla equally kind, was a calm, capable woman who'd left her career as a teacher once their children started arriving. Max loved maple bars and detested exercise. Priscilla was a natural athlete and gifted golfer. Though I was fond of Max, I became more and more drawn to Priscilla's company, and she graciously enveloped me into her large circle of friends.

I chose, rather than joining in her church groups or community volunteering, to create times when it was just Priscilla and me who would have coffee in her kitchen with outlooks on Bellingham Bay, or the two of us taking my kids to the park. Priscilla was always receptive to any activity, and her heart was open to all. We appointed her and Max "godparents" of my son James, though it was an informal title.

Priscilla was one of those listeners who was always totally focused on whomever was speaking. She made me feel as if I were the most interesting person in the world. And, when she was with James, he naturally felt the same way. He couldn't articulate her magic, but simply wanted to spend time with her whenever possible. I loved how he, a rather shy boy, seemed to flourish in her company.

When I had to return to teaching part time when my son was five, I was loath to put him in any of the daycare options available. He was quiet, not rough and tumble, and I worried he'd get swallowed up or bullied by the masses. I selfishly and bravely asked Priscilla if she would care for him on my teaching days a few times a week. I was sad to be returning to work and leaving my last born, and I didn't think she'd be open for such a commitment. Nonetheless, I brazenly made my request. Deep inside, I knew it was unfair to ask; she'd raised five children and now enjoyed her well-deserved free time. But this was my boy, and I wanted the best for him. I prayed that she'd accept, and somehow that stunning combination Mary Poppins and Buddha agreed, saying she'd *love* to spend extra time with her godson.

I'm sure those hours James spent with Priscilla were more fun, more open ended and more empowering than any he spent with me. From the moment he walked through her front door, *he* decided what they would do that day. Whereas I was strict about candy and sugared cereals, Priscilla kept a fresh box of Kix & Honey, his absolute favorite (forbidden at home) with full, ongoing access whenever he wanted. When I'd pick him up, eager for his company, I noted how reluctantly he left Priscilla's side. I came to envy her children for what must have been the best possible childhood one could imagine; a kindly, quiet father and an endlessly energetic and enthusiastic companion and cheerleader as a mother.

As my children grew up, our family remained close to both Max and

Priscilla. My son had his one year of bliss with Priscilla as his playmate a couple of days a week, and that extraordinary time they spent contributed greatly to his sense of self. Though both my kids loved the couple, it was clear there was a special bond between her and James.

When James was twelve, Priscilla became ill with colon cancer. Max had died, also of cancer, a few years earlier, and I know she missed him terribly. Over the many months she was ill, I was able to see her several times a week, already grieving the changes the disease wrought. Occasionally, my children would come for short visits, but Priscilla's energy was waning. The number of people who communicated with her and provided food and support wasn't surprising, but it was impressive. At her funeral, there were several hundred people, and I wouldn't doubt that each one felt she was their special friend.

A couple of weeks before she passed away, Priscilla asked for me to bring James to say good-bye. I worried for him that it would be too tough, and was concerned for Priscilla's emotional state, but she insisted, and James was strangely willing.

When we arrived, Priscilla was lying on the couch, clearly in pain but with her standard cheerful demeanor. She pulled James close and gave him a tender hug. Then, she said to my boy, still a boy, but on the brink of his journey to becoming a teenager, "You are wonderful, wonderful young man, and I know someday you will be the best husband and father. Having a family is the most important job in our lives. I promise, you will love having your own children to care for, and a partner to go through life with. I love you, and love what you've been for me in my life."

It was such an extraordinary thing to say to someone my son's age. I remember being surprised that Priscilla chose to speak of that time, far in the future for James, but retrospectively I understood; family is everything, and that includes the family you choose. James took in her words with a nearly holy acceptance, suddenly maturing in the moment, clearly understanding the magnitude of what was being said, and the poignancy of the context of the situation.

They hugged again, such a tender hug, and I, heart aching and tears flowing, took my son out of a home that helped to form the best of him. He is now a wonderful husband and father, just as Priscilla predicted.

Friends who bring treasured times and value to our existence are exceptional. Those who do so in the lives of our beloved children are cherished beyond measure. To this day, I often talk to Priscilla, wonder what she would advise, and tell her of her godson's happy life. I've tried, also, to emulate her inclusive, loving nature with two boys who became my unofficial godsons. Priscilla modeled the concept that there's always more love, more time, and more reason to care for a child, a person, or someone who, without realizing it, needed an example of how to be their best self.

She was that shining example for me, and for all who knew her. Though she died far too early, the force of her love remains here on earth within her friends and family, and deep inside that lucky boy who was always treated to Kix & Honey.

17

Mary and Michelle

MENTORSHIP

The delicate balance of mentoring someone is not creating them in your own image, but giving them the opportunity to create themselves.

—Steven Spielberg

A few years after Priscilla died, I made several changes in my life. I had been wanting to switch careers for some time, and I was leaving my marriage. Those two gigantic transitions happened somewhat simultaneously, and both would prove to be life changing beyond the obvious.

I had been an educator for nearly twenty years but yearned to work in the field of communications and marketing. I was particularly interested in what was called video production in those days, but I had no training. I read a lot of books and screenplays, then did more reading about how to do public relations and marketing. At that time, there *were* computers, but they were just beginning to be incorporated into our homes and were not the tools for endless information and access they are now, so books were my primary source of information.

Still teaching, but wanting to implement the career change, I approached my son's karate instructor and asked if I could create a marketing campaign for him for free. I needed the experience, he could benefit from additional students, and free was—free. He kindly agreed, and every night, I would pore over those marketing books from the library, taking notes. I copied ideas for general strategies, wrote out a plan, and started his—and my—first marketing outreach.

It was, if not wildly successful, promising and did help his business. So I asked another small business owner if I could do the same for him. Then another.

There was an organization of women in communication in our community—I think that was actually the title of the group—and I learned what day and time they had their meetings. So I bolstered my confidence and forced myself to show up at their next scheduled gathering. I knew no one in the field, had no idea what and how the organization worked, but I was hungry to gain as much information as possible in any way possible.

All the women in the room were friendly and interested in my venture. No one laughed at me, at least to my face, for my bold and uneducated ambition. Then, a couple women took me under their wing.

Mary and Michelle were both successful practitioners of their craft. They'd been working in the field for many years and had an educational background that clearly contributed to their expertise. They, separately and together, began meeting with me and coaching me in my new field. Suggestions were offered and ideas provided. Support was constant. I took everything they gave me and implemented the ideas as fully as I could.

Eventually, I was able to leave teaching and begin my second career as a marketing consultant. The first few years were definitely the "fake it till you make it" approach, but I couldn't have faked anything if I hadn't had two legitimate professionals by my side.

I worked for several years as an independent consultant, then took a fabulous job as a writer/producer at our local television station. My primary responsibility was to market the video production arm of the company, then write and produce promotional and informational videos.

Five years earlier, sitting in the middle of a classroom, overrun by seven-year-olds and coming home so exhausted I had to take a long bath every night to recover before I could summon energy for my own children, I never would have imagined such a dramatic change in my work life. As hard as I worked at my new job, at the end of the day I was energized, rather than drained. This was where I wanted to be, and I was lucky enough to have found my way there.

Could I have transitioned as successfully without Mary and Michelle? I doubt it. Their generous contribution of time, shared skills, and unwavering support of my dream was a new experience for me. They would become personal friends, but they were not when they offered to help. Their skill set was always better than mine, more finessed, and informed, but they kindly and openly let me into a club I was aching to join.

This was my first experience of women supporting women professionally, and it, indeed, changed my life. When I was an educator, there was always support, but our tasks were delineated, and we all had to have the same skill set before we set foot in a classroom.

The world of business was completely different. I came late to the game, with no training and no expertise. But I learned and grew because of the mentoring I received. I know that now women mentoring women is flourishing in all arenas, but my experience so many years ago was of such generosity and kindness, it qualifies as something more; another brand of friendship.

18

Robin

HEARTBREAKING LESSON

*On the death of a friend, we should consider that the fates through
confidence have devolved on us the task of a double living, that we
have henceforth to fulfill the promise of our friend's life also, in our
own, to the world.*

—Henry David Thoreau

Another woman from the communications group was Robin. She
was, in terms of appearances, a total mismatch to the group. Most
came to these evening meetings in their work clothes, which were overall fairly conservative. Hairstyles matched the outfits, with trimmed,
bobbed hair or, if long, contained in proper, slicked ponytails. Robin,
on the other hand...

I've never met anyone, nor had a close friend, who had as singular an
appearance as Robin, and only one other pal, my fastidious Fran, who
had a laugh that could compete. Robin had an earth mother body, with
very large breasts, rounded limbs and unhinged, bright yellow long hair
that leapt halfway down her back. She always wore bright red lipstick—
and this was before red lipstick was worn by anyone but our mothers.
But the sight of this ready-for-battle warrior body, flowing locks and

ruby mouth that was not only red, but constantly barking guffaws—was irresistible.

Robin also was in the field, but not the trenches like Michelle and Mary. She wrote columns for a very small community newspaper, trying to expand her freelance work. Her usual day job was, as I recall, in administration of a business office.

She was married to Michael, an artist, and they had chosen to be childless. Michael was an adequate artist who never had any success but was committed to his work, so it was Robin who supported the couple all the years they were married. She believed in him, and had the temperament to be the breadwinner, though I know at times it tried her patience.

Occasionally, Michael would take a job as a part time housepainter, and it was on one of those infrequent posts that he fell from the top of a ladder, hit his head, and died a few days later. He was only fifty.

The loss was, of course, devastating for Robin. It had been the two of them together for over twenty years, and now she was a widow. They'd always struggled monetarily, and the costs of Michael's hospital and funeral expenses brought more financial strain. But Robin soldiered on.

Besides going to movies or plays with Robin—who always enjoyed the humor more than anyone and could jumpstart a collective chuckle in a huge theater via her own joyful, roaring laugh—my favorite activity with her was Queen's night. This was a once a month gathering of Robin, our friend Andrea, and myself. We would open a bottle of wine, Robin would make or bring a stunningly delicious pear and gorgonzola pizza (she was a fabulous cook) and Andrea, who *still* barely cooks, would, under our strict super vision, try to put together a salad for the three of us.

After social visiting, wine and pizza, we would gather in the living room of whoever's house it was. Then, one of us would bring out the "crown"—something that Robin had found for our purpose—and that person would place the crown on their head and begin to present a work and/or career issue to the other two. Brainstorming, support, out-of-the-box and in-the-box solutions would be forthcoming. Then, the crown would go to the next woman until all three of us had had a turn at presenting our challenge. Everyone got a turn, even if it took us late into the night.

Though the professional group where I met Robin was wonderful, there was something organic and heart-running earnest in our Queen Night trio. Robin was at the core of it; not just because of her pizza, but her exuberant personality, willingness to learn and explore in her own work practices, and, that laugh. The laugh was always at the ready; loud, and an instant day-maker.

A few years after Michael died, Robin began to quietly complain about not feeling well. She did not have health insurance, and said repeatedly, when I would urge her to see a doctor, that she couldn't afford the one hundred dollars a month for the cost of insurance, or for a doctor's visit. She was very into alternative medicine and pursued treatments in that realm, feeling better for a bit, then not. She would not accept money from me for insurance—even to start a policy.

After several months, when she got too uncomfortable, Robin finally saw a physician and was diagnosed with ovarian cancer. She died within the year.

Her death, and the loss of that enormous and captivating energy, took a great toll on all who knew and loved her. My takeaway lesson was, if anyone I knew was again not able to afford insurance, I would *insist* and assist in helping them to find a way to get coverage.

Many years later, I had a chance to do so with my two godsons, and I know they grew weary of my haranguing them to get coverage. But the fact that Robin might have been saved or had her life extended had she received medical attention sooner, and consequently that laugh, those laughing lips, that wild blond hair and extraordinary spirit are gone forever—that's a horrible and profound lesson.

Once, several years after Robin passed away, I was on an airplane and saw, amazingly, a flight attendant who was her doppelganger. The hair, the body type—even the red lips. I'd never seen anyone who looked *close* to the strong and vibrant presence of Robin. I was so startled, I approached the woman and remarked on her resemblance to my friend, though I didn't mention she wasn't living. The woman was kind, and we chatted a bit, I, fighting every urge to hug her in recognition.

Robin had always been very spiritually inclined, and a part of me likes to believe she managed that random visit as a gift. If not, it was still an offering from *somewhere*, and I was grateful for the moment and remembrance. That's what grand and good comrades bring, whether still present or now gone. It's that layer, and depth of connection—a testament to the extraordinary power of friendship.

19

Andrea

SOLO DOESN'T MEAN LONELY

I'm an introvert. If your party isn't better than the one in my head, I'm not interested.

—John Mark Green

Knowing the third "queen", Andrea, has been an education. As distinctive as Robin was in appearance and personality, it was Andrea who set the bar for being unusual in lifestyle and priorities. She is different than any other close friend. And when I say "close", there are brackets around the word, because Andrea defines the parameters of interactions with others on her own terms.

Andrea's definition of a "perfect life" is radically different than most of my pals. Typically, my close female acquaintances have been married at one point or another; or, single and frustrated with never having found that "right" partner. Many have children. Andrea has never married; never even came close. She's had only a couple relationships. She's extremely attractive and bright but not on the same trajectory as my other single friends or acquaintances.

The key to her contentment? A defined formula for a socially skilled, yet self-delighted introvert.

I've been fascinated by Andrea's developmental arc over the two decades I've known her. When we met, she, like Robin and I, was trying to get a marketing position with an established business. She definitely had the required skill set. When we celebrated "Queen's Night", she always had the most up to date information about our field and cutting-edge suggestions for our professional challenges. She presents well and was always astute in her analysis of potential employer's needs. She'd be offered jobs, do the work, but never feel content leaving her house and working under someone else's roof. It just wasn't her style and was counter to her natural inclination to work and live solo.

Over the years, she's figured out how to work for herself as a media consultant and Twitter maven, now very active in the Bikes for Climate and Plant Based for Climate movements and with an international reputation.

I have come to regard Andrea as her own nation; fully capable of self-governing, willing to cooperate with others and contribute, but most content to attend her own parades and celebrations.

She does *not* present as an introvert. She talks a lot, and she talks *really fast.* I used to assume that, because she doesn't speak with many people during the day, when she *does* interact with others, she has a lot stored up and she has to push it all out. Nope. It's just her conversational style.

I also present as an extrovert, but am, in fact, an introvert with excellent social skills. While I am a pleaser, Andrea is pleasant, but her top priority is pleasing herself. Her ideal day is a two to three-hour bike ride, two long walks with her two dogs, work, and chatting with her beloved parents who live half a country away. True, she is constantly interacting online with clients and folks she is connected to via her special interests but being without face-to-face human contact all day suits her best.

When Andrea chooses to be with someone it's super charged, but the sessions are limited. If we have dinner, the unspoken time frame is just a little over an hour. We eat, talk quickly, discussing films, books and media, with some personal information exchanged. Then, usually suddenly she'll say, "Well, thanks. This has been great. Send me a link to such and such." She'll stand quickly, put on her bicycle helmet, and prepare to ride miles in the dark, pointed toward the small house she has rented for years, her beloved dogs awaiting her return.

The first several occasions she declared our socialization over before I had thought it was kosher, I was a bit insulted, assuming my company and/or contribution to the conversation wasn't stimulating. But that's not it. Andrea has a "people" limit, and no matter how much she cares about someone, and I *know* she cares about me, she reaches a certain threshold of intake and she's *done*.

Once I was familiar with and understood her pattern, I started giving myself permission to follow some of her practices. That was the initial lesson in boundaries she modeled; leave when you want to—it's not necessary to work within the standard protocol. I began considering the possibility that I, too, didn't need to be the "good girl" with perfect social skills, always accommodating others. I could be the "good to me" woman who valued my time and energy above a prescribed set of norms. Yes, I could enjoy coffee with a friend, but it didn't have to be two hours when I really would have preferred that second hour for time alone.

Now, I listen more to myself, and honor myself with increased grace, because of Andrea's example. Her life has narrow boundaries that bring her tremendous happiness. My life now incorporates parameters I'd never applied before, and the emotional and psychological benefits have been significant. It's Andrea I'll call when I'm afraid I'm being taken advantage of so she can give me the proper perspective, and it's Andrea I require to set me straight if I find my backbone bending too quickly.

It's one of life's treats when the teacher isn't the one you think she'll be, and the lessons ones you didn't know you needed, until you find yourself changed. Andrea's role, by example, helped me develop a certain practice of self-care that has often healed my soul and strengthened my emotional core.

20

Book Club

SOUL SISTERS

What's the point of having a book club if you don't get to eat brownies and drink wine?

—Jami Attenberg, "*The Middlesteins*

W hen I was newly divorced, I was invited into my first book club. I've been a member of several since; the book club made up of scientists who didn't drink; the book club of friends I know socially that's pretty serious about discussions; the book club that chats about books but prefers to debate about politics. That first book club is the one where, after the first year, we never talked about books. It's also the one that's been my emotional and psychological lifeline for over twenty years.

I've written about this group before (in my memoir "How I Learned I'm Old"). Because that was largely a humorous book, there were all sorts of disclosures about the racy things the club discussed. I won't repeat those anecdotes here, but the most important takeaway I'll transfer is that, in nearly twenty-five years, we only discussed books *the first year* we met, and *never again.*

So, what did those six women do all those years, meeting once a month, telling our partners and children we'd be occupied for the next three hours, and might require a designated driver by the end of the evening? We unfolded our souls.

Until my mid-forties, I'd not been a part of a "group" beside that first one in junior high and the Communications organization, but the latter was professional and the former—well, it was junior high. I'm not a group person normally, though I seem to have acquired a couple meaningful ones the past ten years. But until "Book Club", I'd never met with women I hadn't known and made a commitment to continue gathering for what now appears to be for the rest of my life.

I only knew one woman when I joined. She'd invited two others, who invited two others. On paper, I didn't have much in common with most, either personally or professionally. The friend who invited me had been a theatre pal, but it was her boyfriend who was the actor and I the actress. She always seemed nice, but I didn't *know* her, even, at that point, as a close friend. A few of us had children; two did not. Some married, some divorced, some single at one point or another. Two women worked for city government, the rest of us professionally diverse.

What happened over the next two decades that made me stay committed to that particular group? I've quit other clubs with people I had more in common with than this group. And, I've certainly enjoyed discussing books more in other groups as, after our initial few meetings, we never raised the subject again. What was clear was that, we, a group of women then in our thirties and forties, somehow established a level of emotional safety in our conversation. That mysterious connection enabled us to provide a strong, constant support for all the life circumstances that would happen to each of us in the upcoming decades.

And a lot occurred: divorces, breakups, crises with children, parents who were aging, then failing, then dying. With each woman and every issue, the feedback, empathy and understanding that was offered built, then added upon, a foundation of unparalleled trust. Every woman brought something unique to the group; Coni, one of those "cute her whole life" women who might be annoying if she weren't so dear, always contributed an unerring wisdom to discussions; Adele, from a large Italian family, modeled loyalty and commitment to tribe and friends; Sue K, constantly injected the group with joyous zest for fun and new experiences and was *always* the last to bed and last to rise; Sue H, who grew up in a small, crowded trailer with many siblings, showed extraordinary thoughtfulness in her emotional processing and in every gift she selected (and there were a lot of birthday celebrations over the years); and Leslie, a recovering alcoholic, provided an example of strength of character that we all admire (though we don't follow her particular model of sobriety).

Was it our diversity, the regularity of meetings, the time in our lives, or some lucky alchemy that made this group of women different from every other "book club?" I've talked to a lot of women about their book clubs, have spoken to clubs upon occasion, and feel as if I've studied the phenomenon extensively. I've even written two television pilots on the subject. (Anecdotally, there are plenty of book clubs that never get around to discussing books. I've discovered that many book club members seem to enjoy food and wine more than the discussion.) But for me, this club that established a level of intimacy about *every last detail* of our lives is one of the dearest treasures in my life. The closeness we formed has a depth of connection so meaningful and unusual that we all feel as if we've been chosen by an otherworldly gathering of spirits to be part of a sacred, select sect.

We're still a motley group. I'm closer to some of the women than others. Two joined me, along with another close friend, (all named Sue— not kidding) on a female only barging trip in France for my sixtieth birthday; piloted and crewed by the four of us. Today, the group has, after a couple moved out of area, formed a conglomeration of part book club, plus the "new girl" from the France trip, that somehow, with two out of state, are now five of us, with that same, undefinable bond. We're actually not "Book Club" anymore; the new matchup is "The Tribe."

This group of females has become my family, my sisters, the core of my heart. We've attended one another's weddings, offered solace and extensive hugs during those divorces and breakups. We show up for funerals of relatives we've never met just because the person grieving the loss is one of our own. We speak truths no one else dares speak, all to promote the best possible life of each member.

Confidences spoken are honored and the melding of spirits unchallenged. We've even planned the formation a group home where the two youngest are tasked with changing the older member's diapers, if it comes to that. But it won't matter, because in one or two decades, we will still have our connection woven from history, revelations and protection. We're the Marines of book clubs.

These days, we're geographically scattered between two cities ninety minutes apart (the conglomeration) and we still manage to connect in person for an overnight on a regular basis. During the pandemic we met once a week via Zoom, wine glasses at the ready, and offered up the lifeblood of our union that, at many times, we all felt was one of the primary forces that moved us through the catastrophe.

Book clubs, for most women who are lucky enough to claim their own, are a mostly female-centric phenomenon world-wide. But *my* first book club—the one that has brought me more laughter, solace, support and entertainment than I ever would have imagined—was a gift somehow delivered on wings of goddesses.

Jeanne

NEIGHBOR IS A VERB

A good neighbor is a found treasure.

—Chinese proverb

I 've lived in many houses and many neighborhoods. Apartments, hotels, suburbia and classic. As a child, I was aware of the role neighbors played, but only because I would observe how and why my parents socialized with those who lived nearby.

Jean, who introduced me to the Oz books and was my first generational friendship, was my mother's dear friend and I benefitted from that connection, but she wasn't a "neighborhood friend". The wife of a couple who lived across the street from my mother and stepfather, who later divorced, introduced me to my second husband thirty years after I knew them slightly as a teenager, but that service, as great as it was, couldn't be regarded as "neighborly." Edie, my first friend when I was five, lived down the block, but I never thought of her as a neighbor; she was a convenient pal whom I met because of proximity. But it wasn't until I was in my fifties that I knew a true, great neighbor.

When I met and married my second husband, I moved into his house after selling my treasured abode in a different city. His was not a home I had chosen, nor did I like much about it, except, ironically, for the neighbors across the street, with whom we enjoyed socializing. I negotiated for moving somewhere we could choose together, and we relocated a few blocks away to a 1914 Craftsman cottage that needed remodeling. Despite a crazy contractor and the typical unpleasant surprises one encounters in such endeavors, we were pleased with the end result.

The day we moved in, however, was horrific. In an effort to save money (will we ever learn?) we'd hired a fly-by-night moving crew of two guys who arrived several hours late, one of whom left midway through the process. Though we were only moving less than a mile away, it still involved packing up a household, manhandling bulky, heavy furniture, and transporting an endless pile of boxes. We'd planned for a five-hour time frame beginning early in the day, but the late start and haphazard movers morphed the plan into a nightmare with my husband and me doing most of the work. Twelve hours later, by seven p.m., we were furious with the situation and physically exhausted. That's when Jeanne showed up with dinner and cookies.

Jeanne was, praise the Lord, our new next-door neighbor. She and her husband David, both charming and brilliant, were, at that time, parents of three equally brilliant boys ranging from six to twelve. But moving night, it was Jeanne, whom we'd never met, who knocked on our door, introduced herself, delivered a hot, delicious dinner and freshly baked cookies, then politely and cheerfully left us to devour the much-needed sustenance.

That introduction was typical of our, and everyone else one the block's, interactions with Jeanne. She provides cookies for the entire neighborhood and every kid at the school bus stop on a regular basis, organizes block parties, entertains legions in her home and has created a sense of neighborhood unprecedented in our current times.

Part of a large family and having grown up in the Midwest, Jeanne was, in all those practices, replicating her childhood experiences of service, friendliness and unending thoughtfulness for those sharing local geography. She explained to me once the pleasure of sitting on the front stoop of her family's house in Chicago and having neighbors socialize day and night. "I don't understand why people in the Northwest don't do that," she remarked. After meeting Jeanne, I don't either, as long as it would be with Jeanne.

Every New Year's Day, Jeanne, an accomplished photographer, (though with her baking skills, she really doesn't need to master anything else), stops by each house on the block, provides hats, crazy beads and glasses with the new year's date on them, and takes a photograph which she prints and later provides to each household. The photos we have from those years are amongst our most treasured, capturing a place in time.

David has been successful in his business endeavors, allowing Jeanne to be the household engineer (though she's returned to school in recent years as the boys have grown). One might think she was a throwback to my parent's generation as the stay-at-home Mom, but that would do a disservice to her skills and contributions. She volunteered at the kid's schools and local service organizations while maintaining an obscenely clean home (three boys?). She is a mother extraordinaire. Her breakfast, lunches and dinners are gourmet feasts. Most days, in the morning long before dawn, she runs with women she's known for decades, then begins a day of cheerful service.

She's funny, gorgeous in the way a fit, no frills or airs beauty can be. The heart of her household and the long block in the area where she's cemented the nearby community, Jeanne is so unusual in character and contribution, I don't even *try* to emulate the model she provides.

After several years in the neighborhood, we left that block and moved into our "final" home, as modern as the prior was charming and dated. Our one hesitation was leaving Jeanne, knowing we'd never have anyone who would replicate the experience of having her next door. We're still friends with Jeanne and David, as is anyone who has ever lived near them. She still bakes cookies daily for anyone who stops by for coffee (she's the only friend I know who has an open-door policy and *loves* drop-ins).

I've always thought of Jeanne much as I view Mr. Rogers. There are just some people who are so good, so evolved and kind, we're just lucky to know them and be within their circle of goodwill. I'm a *slightly* better neighbor to others because of knowing Jeanne, but it's really been the luck of being one of the select recipients of her largesse that makes having her on earth one of life's extraordinary, magical gifts. Like Mr. Rogers.

Liz and Melissa

The evolution of man is the evolution of his consciousness, and consciousness cannot evolve unconsciously. The evolution of man is the evolution of his will, and will cannot evolve involuntarily.

—G.I. Gurdjieff

I've been a member of a writing group for years. We're a motley crew in that we have varied interests and writing styles, experience and expertise, but the group is meaningful to every single member. We appreciate the trust we've built over the years to disclose personal perspectives and opinions. Our critiques are fair and delivered with respect and sensitivity. However, the trust that must be the baseline of those practices has been built up over time. We've had to pay our dues, take one another's measure, and surrender our egos.

The group was started by our friend Marcia, and we're all grateful she brought such disparate souls together. But, at this point, we're not all the original members. We've lost a couple good ones along the way or someone just wasn't a fit. One woman only stayed for one meeting— I think she was surprised we didn't tell her she was the most brilliant writer we'd encountered. A woman would leave; someone would suggest a replacement. Some of agreed; some of us didn't. We stayed static.

After we'd lost a couple women who'd moved away, there was once again some grumbling about replacing them. I voted no; who could say that new people would be worthy of our collective trust? But our fearless leader kept pushing for two women she knew, best friends, and I had to give in to a majority vote. I recall being uneasy about two people coming in together; that was a fifth of our total membership—we'd purposefully kept the group small - and could definitely impact all that was lovely in our interpersonal exchange.

Melissa and Liz arrived for their first meeting with quiet, yet impressive resumes. Both were employees of a local community college; Liz as administration in the Business School and Melissa as an art instructor. Melissa was very petite, with a pixie haircut and dark, dancing eyes. Liz, willowy and exotic with long black hair, had a very different look but, somehow, they felt like a cohesive unit. They immediately endeared themselves to us by expressing their passion for improving their own work and ability to astutely analyze the issues with the individual's presentation.

Their incorporation into the group—the group that I was a part of and had voted "no" on their inclusion in—took just one session. It was as seamless a transition as Julia Child folding egg whites into a souffle.

It's been a number of years since the two dark-haired beauties knocked on Marcia's door. They've shared countless stories and essays, critiqued endless play scenes, anecdotes and poetry, and laughed and teared up with the rest of us when particularly touched by someone's contribution. Their role in the dynamic is remarkable. I *thought* we were complete and didn't need any more members. Then I realized we were desperate for *exactly those two.*

We read our work aloud to the group, and I quickly began to notice that both Liz and Melissa had the ability to connect on a deeper level to whatever piece was being presented. Their comments seemed to be astute in a different way than those of other, equally talented members.

The clear definer for me for both women is that they are extraordinarily thoughtful in how they live their lives. Not "thoughtful" as in

"She gives the nicest gifts." Instead, they have a shared talent for going deeper in their observations and delineating areas that need work or recognizing writing that shines.

The strange thing was, they appeared to have a kind of "twinship" when it came to the depth of their perceptions. I wondered why and how this was so. It wasn't like everyone else in the group was a slouch when it came to perception or analysis. Yet, there was something deeper, more intricate in their process. I decided to interview them to see if I could delineate why. Part of my motivation was my wish to be as thoughtful as they; as "other" centered.

It was a funny process, interviewing friends, but they were both excited to discuss the issues I was raising. It turns out, they *are* very different than me. Better people, more citizens of the world. Less ego.

My questions included the following: Do you start the day with a deliberate intention? Do you think you feel more deeply than other people? Is your ego less than others? What are your deepest values— what matters most? As both women had an opportunity to respond to those and other ancillary questions, I had the chance to compare what my answers would be. It wasn't necessarily humbling, because I was prepared to come up short, but it was an opportunity for me to take a deep look inside and try to recalibrate my values. Here's a summary:

Liz usually takes a quiet moment before a task, particularly in her professional life, as she's recently taken on temporary Dean positions at various community colleges. She then says to herself, "This is not about me." (I, on the other hand, always *want* it to be about me, but force myself to not focus on that wish.) Melissa tries to be completely open to people and circumstances. She's interested in the rest of humanity; their stories, their hearts.

Both women come from a deep sense of gratitude. They enter a situation like our writing group filled with appreciation for the opportunity to hear others' works and to share in that community. (I feel that too, but I can barely *wait* till it's *my* turn to share.) Neither woman thought she felt more deeply than anyone else but expressed a great deal of empathy towards others if they couldn't necessarily express or communicate their feelings. (I just can't seem to get away from feeling that my feelings are deeper than most. They're not.)

Both women said the most important thing in their lives is love. Liz added that "meaning" is part of that. Melissa expressed her philosophy as, "How do we hold one another in as full an embrace as we can, including the earth and animals and everything around us knowing we will be imperfect at it, but it's worth giving it a go." She talked about not needing to feel the need to leave a legacy behind when she dies, but her readiness to "return to air." She, like all of us, doesn't want to be a burden to those she leaves behind, and wants them to understand her appreciation for being on earth, being *of* earth, and wish to leave no imprint behind.

Liz noted that, particularly since Covid, her mantra, when things feel dour and get tough, is "I choose joy."

The interview lasted more than an hour and was filled with extraordinary examples of how both women view themselves and their place in the world. Afterward, I felt like I'd spent an hour with Pema Chodron or some other equally wise soul. Even more grateful for their friendship but also thankful to have two such teachers. We've had many interesting talks, not just about writing, over the years. We discuss books, politics, our perspective on parenting or our community. But this was different.

The impact of our conversation was immediate. I had been feeling badly that a couple people dropped off my email list for my blog—feeling rejected and unappreciated. I could then decide to view my writing as Melissa views her art; "It's something I do just for me", she had remarked. I was reminded that the opinions of others should have nothing to do with why, what or how I write. Melissa also noted she came early to the understanding that, "I'm enough. I'm enough for me." I reflected the insecurity I typically feel of never being enough and vowed to adopt her mantra.

Liz's refrain from her early years as an administrator, "It's not about me" she would say at the beginning of a meeting or day of stress. That also weaves through my consciousness now. The internal shift feels lighter, more *right*.

There was a big surprise after that interview process. I've known these women for years, appreciated them and their notable qualities just as long. But it took a different mode of interaction, a questioning that itself delved deeper than we'd done in our standard interchange, that led to such meaningful insights and inspiration. Something that, in that one hour, changed my way of viewing "self." This peeling back, layering, reminded me that if someone is in my life, I can always go deeper, explore differently, grow more. Another gift of friendship.

22

Sue

LOST AND FOUND

If nature has made you for a giver, your hands are born open, and so is your heart; and though there may be times when your hands are empty, your heart is always full, and you can give things out of that—warm things, kind things, sweet things—help and comfort and laughter.

—Frances Hodgson Burnett, *A Little Princess*

Around the time I met and married my second husband and moved to the little abode next to wonderful Jeanne, I met Sue. I'd done some acting over the years and needed a new head shot. She was the photographer who'd been recommended by industry professionals.

Sue has an unusual version of physical beauty. It's like a pixie met an angel and called it good.

I'd been away from Seattle for nearly thirty years and had no friends in the area. I wasn't looking for a friend the day of the shoot, but our shared interest in acting and one of those spark connections that happen when the universe shines right deemed it so. We started having coffee, going for walks and getting to know one another.

I have friends much younger and much older, so I was never worried that the fifteen years age difference would be an issue in our friendship.

To me, age is the least interesting reason to spend time with someone. Sue had all the qualities I value; great sense of humor, large measures of integrity, a generous heart and the shared joy of being a parent. I must admit, there was one time in the years we've known each other that someone mistook her for my daughter, but she looks very young, and, apparently, I look old for my age. Sigh.

Sue became my best friend in Seattle. For years, we walked together, had dinner frequently, and she joined two other friends (also named Sue) and myself on that barging trip in France for my sixtieth birthday. We called her "The Bait" because, when we approached a lock, if we sent her up front to the bow with her long hair and flirty disposition, the lockmaster would always jump to attention to assist us if needed. She's still "The Bait" any time we walk down the street; there's something about her looks that is so distinct and dreamy, people always stop and stare. She denies this vehemently.

Several years after we'd cemented our close bond, I was disappointed by something Sue had done. The details don't matter, but what does is that I broke off the friendship, heartbroken by what I perceived of as a lack of loyalty or commitment.

Everything shifted. There was a now a huge gap in my life and my heart. I missed her but held on to my anger. She was experiencing her own pain about the "separation." The two other two Sues, caught in the middle, (we called our foursome "The Frenchies" after the France trip and gathered often), now saw each of us separately.

I made new friends, but none brought into my life what Sue had supplied all those years. Although I had, in the past, broken away from a couple of friends for self-preservation, this was different. Sue hadn't deliberately disappointed me, I began to realize, and I acknowledged, at least to myself, that I had been overly sensitive to the situation. I hadn't practiced understanding or forgiveness with someone I knew never meant me harm.

The other two "Frenchies" began to hint at Sue being as sad as I was by our continued rift. Finally, after a couple of years, we tentatively arranged to meet to discuss what had happened. I was more scared about that meeting than I ever was for any date or job interview.

We began our difficult conversation. Tears were shed, understanding began. It would take several more meetings before we returned to the level of intimacy we'd shared before, but the effort we made to reconnect has strengthened the bond of our friendship so deeply it will last as long as we're both on earth. The "Frenchies" still meet, with one addition of Coni, from the original "Book Club". This group is so close and committed to one another, we're a band of sisters from different mothers.

My lesson from the challenge of having such a great friend, then losing her, was to view this experience as a big, fat, life lesson. Sometimes, being right isn't the most important thing, and I *love* being right. Sometimes, you just need to get quiet and pay attention to intention rather than action. Sometimes, second chances at love, and that's exactly what this is—love—are given, and only an idiot turns her back on those kinds of chances. There's no doubt I'm still an idiot about many things, but knowing Sue, losing Sue, and having her return to my life has made me smarter about what really matters. Intention. Forgiveness. Love.

23

Janet

OF THE EARTH

You must live in the present, launch yourself on every wave, find your eternity in each moment. Fools stand on their island opportunities and look toward another land. There is no other land, there is no other life but this.

—Henry David Thoreau

Friends support, entertain, sustain and challenge. Sometimes, they inspire awe. That's Janet.

I have written about Janet before, but she's worth a chapter. In fact, she's worth a book, but this will have to do for now. The chapter about her in my book is entitled "What Would Janet Do?" That's the mantra my writing group has adopted after being in Janet's company for many years. We have learned that whenever we have any kind of challenge; physical, emotional or mental, to ask that question and imagine Janet's response. Then we try to match it as best as we can, though I think all would agree we can't touch her courage or attitudinal levels.

Janet has had cancer many times. She lives with the reality that cancer might show up in her body again tomorrow. She is closer to eighty than seventy, and she is a fighter, a warrior, of the first order. She has survived a marriage with a mentally ill husband, challenges with her two children and repercussions of treatments for the disease. It's astounding, truly astounding, that she's still on this earth.

She's not just *on* the earth, though. She's *of* the earth in that she is as powerful as a force of nature. Whatever happens in her body or her life, she simply bursts through it, finds the best of the situation, and goes *there*. She doesn't wallow. Nor does she indulge in self-pity or anger. No matter what physical challenge confronts her, she acknowledges it calmly, addresses the solution and immediately implements whatever action needs to take place. No drama.

Janet is *not* the Pollyanna version of a positive attitude. It's inherent in her spirit; almost like she can't help herself. She simply—and how can this be simple—notices and appreciates each and every miracle in her life and focuses on *that*.

Despite having to travel with four suitcases filled with sustenance for her feeding port that she must attach to *every single night*; despite ongoing and chronic diarrhea due to damage done from radiation, despite broken bones and failed systems throughout her body, Janet gets on airplanes (pre-pandemic) and travels to wherever she finds joy. She snorkels, although her doctor prefers she would not because of her port, but snorkeling fills that warrior body with bliss, and Janet always chooses bliss.

And when Janet loves, she *loves*. She's very attached to two great nieces and revels in their company. She loves her friends fiercely, her sons passionately, and her partner with steadfast acceptance and appreciation.

I've always been a neurotic worrier, someone who immediately focuses on the negative before I sit myself down and attempt to reroute my psyche. I'll never be able to do anything but try to emulate Janet's "can do" attitude, particularly when it comes to health challenges. Most of the time, I fail. But there's another other gift Janet has modeled that I *have* been able to practice more regularly since knowing her: a love and appreciation for the beauty of the natural world.

Whether it's at her beloved cabin on Puget Sound or walking through a city park, Janet sees and notices gifts of nature. The patterns of bark on a tree. The iridescent shading on a shell or the way the mist settles itself like a whisper atop saltwater. It's as if Janet is so attuned to the core of life that she has a direct dial to its essence. I've been in her presence enough times to witness her spiritual and physical relationship to nature and its gifts. Now, whenever I am outdoors, I pay attention more, stop more, listen and breathe more. Because of that gift she has of connection to the molecules and cells that surround us from earth's bounty, I, like a pupil at the feet of Buddha, have begun to witness the silent, stunning offerings that Janet communes with in such a organic way.

Would she have this gift if she *hadn't* suffered such physical tests and indignities? I believe so, but the juxtaposition of her mystical connection to nature with the physical and emotional valor she exemplifies is truly awe-inspiring. We're all blessed to know her and will continue to aspire to follow her example. In spirit, in practice, and in nature.

24

Nina

And now here is my secret, a very simple secret: It is only with the heart that one can see rightly; what is essential is invisible to the eye.

—Antoine de Saint-Exupéry, *The Little Prince*

F inding a friend late in life, a beloved friend, is tricky. Though I have been lucky enough to acquire a few, I'm always surprised to feel close to someone with no shared history, or often, with very little in common. As Nina said to me once we realized we cared about one another, "I didn't think I needed another friend. Then I met you."

Nina and I met on the tennis court, but she doesn't play tennis anymore. She's a triathlete, and I can't imagine anything less joyful than *that* endeavor. She cooks every meal with joy and energy; I prefer to have others take over the task. And though we've been friends for a few years, we're still at the tip of learning about one another's innermost thoughts. We don't have heart-to-hearts. Most of our socialization is with our husbands, yet we're dear buddies. The only way I can describe *why* we're friends is that, for some reason, we captured one another's hearts.

I'm not sure why I secured hers, but I know why she captured mine.

I love my women friends for various reasons; they set an example, enlighten me, inspire me or support me. Some make me laugh. Others help me grow as a person. But Nina? She just loves me.

She's very tiny. You would be too, if you exercised forty-three hours a day. She's short but is not just petite; she's all muscle. The largest muscle within that mighty body is her heart. Despite her size, it's as if that specific organ contains her body rather than her body being the house of her heart.

She's a rabid competitor in the sports she attacks, and she loves more fiercely than anyone I've known. It would not surprise me to see Nina take down a full-sized bear if it were threatening someone she cared about. The depth of her generosity in energy and commitment to friendship is somewhat Herculean.

Two years ago, she took it upon herself to begin an annual joint birthday party for myself and our mutual friend Gail. Our birthdays are a day apart. The planning that goes into this event would put the entire staff of the Royal Family to shame. Nina and her twin, Carolyn, discuss the offerings. Then they *test* the meal. Sometimes they test it *again*. The dinner is always *fabulous*, but the look on Nina's face as she presents her masterpiece is even better than her superlative meal. She glows just from the joy of doing it for us.

Nina and Carolyn are identical twins, and sometimes I wonder if that's the genesis of Nina's capacity for love. They are extraordinarily close and have been throughout their seventy-five plus years. Reveling in the gift of their twinhood, they speak several times a day on the phone, vacation together and see one another frequently. If you're at a party with the two of them, it's a little like being with newlyweds. There *are* other people in the room, but they are drawn to one another like magnets. I guess they *are* genetic magnets.

Perhaps that gift of intimacy beyond what most of us can imagine, even if one has siblings, is what formed Nina's heart. Maybe all those endorphins she gets from running, swimming and bicycling every day clears out a certain kind of pathway to kindness and generosity.

Anyone who has been chosen to be in her inner circle receives the same caliber of devotion as I get. That doesn't bother me. It's sort of like being on vacation in Hawaii, my favorite spot for a getaway. That sun, the caressing wind that transports you to the beach like an invisible magic carpet—there's nothing that dilutes the experience. I don't mind that I share it all with everyone else on the island. I'm just blissed out I get to be there too. That's what it's like being inside Nina's circle.

Most of us choose dear friends for a reason. But with Nina, all the categories fall away. What's left is that huge heart in the minuscule body. Unexplained in a way, otherworldly in another, but singularly sustaining.

25

Lisa

JUDGING BY THE COVER—BIG MISTAKE

Our universe grants every soul a twin—a reflection of themselves—the kindred spirit—and no matter where they are or how far away they are from each other—even if they are in different dimensions, they will always find one another.

—Julie Dillard

Several years ago, we bought a little beach house in a small community. The houses were very close together, (we eventually moved when a new neighbor bought the house behind us and the six-foot separation became distasteful for several reasons) and all the owners shared a common beach. The place was funky but cozy, and the folks we'd meet on weekends when we ventured up for escape from the city were diverse.

Our neighbors directly across the narrow street, Lisa and Russell, were always friendly. Russell's daughter rented the house below us, so we became familiar with their family on walks or "over the fence" casual conversations.

Lisa and Russell had grown up in the area, had a crush on one another in high school and, forty years later, after marriages with others, reconnected and married. They are wild about one another.

When we met, my husband and I enjoyed them both, though the only clear commonality in terms of background or life experience was that my husband and Russell both played golf. Russell is crazy-friendly, with what he would call a $#!+-eating grin on his face all the time. I thought Lisa was nice, but I didn't have any interest in talking with her outside of the standard neighbor-to-neighbor chat. She seemed like a country girl; in fact, she *was* a country girl, and I am all city. She's an outdoor, horse-riding/owning gal who lived, at that time, on a small farm when they weren't at their cottage. Her idea of a good time is toiling in the garden all morning after a long ride in the hills on her horse, then doing manual labor somewhere else on the property in the afternoon. I'm (pre-pandemic) the opposite; a walk or tennis, work awhile in my indoor office, then choose another indoor activity for the rest of the day.

For a couple of years, we would see the two heading out on their boat to go shrimping or crabbing or doing repairs around their house. Then, one year when we were in California for the winter, Russell and Lisa were in town attending a golf tournament. Out of politeness more than anything else, I invited them for dinner. We had a nice time, and I found myself enjoying talking with Lisa. We still didn't appear to have a lot in common, but I liked her sparky personality and openness to wherever the conversation meandered. Lisa tells me that I said something that day that made her think we might be on the same wavelength, but I don't recall.

That next summer, though we'd moved away from that community, she and I tentatively decided to meet near the old beach house for a picnic lunch. I was a little nervous, as I didn't think we read the same books, shared any common interests, or were even politically aligned. We both had two grown kids, so if the conversation got awkward, there was always that.

Then, somehow, as we unpacked our lunches, the discussion led to spiritual practices. I'm a quiet, "meditate/pray/study consciousness" kind of person, something I only share with my "old" Book Club. That group, over the years, could get, as my friend Kenneth used to say, "Woo

Woo" when someone was having an issue and needed extra support. But I certainly don't discuss my patchwork belief system with other close friends. For one thing, it's a private activity, and people tend to have strong feelings about others who don't share their basic religious tenets or practices. I've always been open to all, and love that most of us in the world get to choose how we connect to a higher power, if that's our need and wont, but I still keep that opinion to myself.

But here was Lisa, the country, hard-working, blue-collar back-grounded woman freely espousing her interests in various books I had quietly pored over, not really having anyone to discuss the premises or practices with after completing the read. I think my jaw dropped onto the picnic table. It was like I'd been living in a foreign country for years, never learning or speaking the language, then overheard someone talking in my mother tongue. That relief of finally being able to *talk!*

That was the beginning of what has been one endless conversation we pick up and leave off whenever we see one another. I might offer something Lisa has passed on to members of the old Book Club if pertinent, but it's really our shared interest in being our best selves through ongoing study and practice that I find to be such an extraordinary gift. And it's Lisa, hard-working, country Lisa that leads lazy me on the quest for new ideas and outlooks.

My cousin Adele is a strong Mormon, and I have learned from her the joy of community through shared religion that church has brought into her life. I have other friends who attend Temple or different denominations and receive the same connection. But it's different when your religious practice is as hodgepodge as mine. It becomes more of a secret; a vitally important piece of yourself that most who are near and dear don't know anything about, and, to be honest, really don't *want* to know. Our belief systems are our own spiritual DNA's business. So, to have discovered that Lisa views everything, and I mean *everything,* through the same lens as I seems like one of those Woo-Woo gifts of the universe.

Sometimes you find a friend you can be totally emotionally naked with, requiring one hundred percent trust and a measure of intimacy that's hard to find. But I never would have imagined that such a person would have come in the package it did, the circumstances as serendipitous, the surprise of discovering her such a delight. That's the kaleidoscope of friendship. We connect with others in so many ways; it's not like we ever have to choose just *one* friend like we select one partner/spouse at a time. The rainbow of colors contained within the facets of that kaleidoscope are brilliant and varied.

Occasionally, you connect with someone who goes beyond the colors and sees your own pure, white light. Isn't it grand that the possibility is always there to discover such a person? Pay attention. You never know when they're about to step into your life.

26

Roberta

LESSONS IN LOVE

Real love means loving kindness and compassion, the kind of love that
does not have any conditions.

—Nhat Hanh, Vietnamese monk

When I was eleven, my parents were divorced. My father had a couple of girlfriends, both of whom I met and liked, but the relationships didn't last. Then, when I was thirteen, I met Roberta, who was to be in my father's life until his death.

She is only ten years older than me and was seventeen years younger than my father. A flight attendant (my father was a pilot), Roberta was quiet, petite, and very athletic. Initially I didn't take to her as I had to girlfriend number one, but over the years I came to appreciate her calm, capable manner. She was a companion in every sense to my father; they skied, sailed, hiked and camped together—all activities that were anathema to my mother. Roberta followed my dad from house to house, state to state, as had my mother, in his quest for the right place that would resonate with his specific requirements for well-being.

My dad did not have a constant state of well-being. He was, in fact, a tortured soul in many ways, and to be his partner meant managing the repercussions of living with a highly charismatic, yet introspective man who meant well but whose demons often tended to have the upper hand.

He was very critical, including of himself. We had a complicated relationship, tempered by the fact that he lived two states away and I only saw him perhaps once or twice a year for decades. On those visits, I observed his appreciation of Roberta's great qualities; her athleticism, openness to new experiences and great organizational skills. But often he just couldn't suppress that greatest demon; his critical self. There were many times I heard a judgement I felt was exaggerated or an emphasis on some small lapse that no one else would have noticed. Roberta always heard such comments with a laugh and patient smile. And though I know he loved her, the devotion she showed him appeared to me to be at a higher level of, well, consciousness, because of his inability to release that inner critic.

They had a great group of friends where they lived near San Diego, and my father was the heart of the group. Handsome, bright and witty, it was like he held court every time they gathered in their condo or on Friday nights for dancing and socializing. And Roberta was there, beside him but always allowing him the spotlight.

They lived together for a couple of decades before they finally married; my father debonair in his white jacket and Roberta looking like a beautiful jewel in her short white designer dress. I have my theories about why they married after all that time, and have no idea if Roberta wanted to marry earlier. I was glad, though, that she could claim the legal and social status of wife. She deserved it.

Then, when my father was in his early seventies, he was diagnosed with Parkinson disease. This was a man who exercised at least two hours a day, didn't have a shred of fat on his body and had always been conscientious about his health.

Roberta, of course, was beside him in the journey that would prove to be embarrassing for my always fit father; distressing and deadly. Continuing to operate a home front that was always clean and tidy and meals that were the envy of all who knew them, Roberta began, over the years of his disease, to take care of more and more of the details of their lives.

My dad was from the "Greatest Generation", and he handled his disease with the dignity typical of men who had fought in that war and returned to begin a new life with the unique understanding that war brings to those who fought and survived the ordeal. But, as he began to lose physical, then mental capabilities, I saw something else happen. He learned to love, truly love, in a way I'd not witnessed before.

The kindness and patience Roberta exemplified minute by minute, year by year, was extraordinary. My dad might have been easy for her to manage before the disease because she loved him so much, but the situation itself, plus the challenges of becoming more and more of a caregiver, had to have been excruciating. Yet Roberta maintained her usual cheerful, loving and efficient self as my father became less and less of himself. But his essence was there, and I began to see something in his eyes as they interacted. It was a pure reflection of the unconditional love Roberta had given him all those years.

I don't know, because I never talked with my father about this, if he ever spoke of the deepening love and appreciation I could see every time I visited them. I hope he did, but I also know that Roberta somehow understood the growth he had made as a person as they progressed through that horrific decline. They still laughed. They went on outings and entertained. And when my father became confused, Roberta gently guided him through situation after situation. And the love grew. That transformation was an extraordinary gift for my father, and I was so touched to see that demon critic be replaced by a pure and loving heart.

My dad passed away fourteen years ago. Roberta and I continue to be in one another's lives, and I regard her as my good friend, though that title of "stepmother", despite the closeness in our ages, adds something special to the relationship. She has a wonderful man in her life who I like and appreciate, and I'm so happy they found each other.

I married a man eight years older than me while my father was still alive but unable to attend our wedding. And though my husband is in great health, the likelihood of me becoming a caregiver in the near future seems a strong possibility. Though I regard myself as a loving partner, I also know that my patience, if I'm placed in that position, will be tested. I like my time to myself and being highly independent, and that's not on the table once someone becomes ill. But I know, when and if that circumstance arrives in our lives, that because of Roberta my friend, and Roberta, the wife of my father, that I will always aspire to be my higher self, patient and loving and endlessly kind.

That gift is one that came from family and is enhanced by friendship. Ultimately, the modeling of the best of being human was provided by example, and I will honor it with reverence and practice.

EPILOGUE

F riendship, it turns out, isn't just one thing, one person, or one level of connection. The women in this book are like a long strand of invisible jewels embedded in my soul. Some are pearls. Some are diamonds. Some glisten and glow, others whisper or shout. Each made their mark. They have, in fact, formed me.

It's an extraordinary gift of humanity—friendship—and one we often take for granted. I hope these chapters have reminded you of the people in your life who made a difference, whose souls and psyches bled into your soul.

Now, go and tell them so.

Made in United States
North Haven, CT
02 August 2022

22123410R00086